At SCOTLAND'S EDGE

'There is scarce a deep sea light from the Isle of Man to North Berwick, but one of my blood designed it. The Bell Rock stands monument for my grandfather; the Skerry Vhor for my uncle Alan; and when the lights come out along the shores of Scotland, I am proud to think that they burn more brightly for the genius of my father.'

ROBERT LOUIS STEVENSON

At
SCOTLAND'S EDGE

*A celebration of two hundred years
of the lighthouse service in Scotland
and the Isle of Man*

Photographs and text by Keith Allardyce
Historical introduction by Evelyn M. Hood

COLLINS
GLASGOW AND LONDON

Keith Allardyce would like to dedicate this book to all
the people of the Northern Lights for their help and
hospitality. Special thanks to Commander John M. Mackay
and the Commissioners for Northern Lighthouses and to
John Clark, Administration Officer, for his guidance
throughout the project, and Inger Anneberg Jacobsen, and
James W. Murray. For their patient generous help Evelyn
Hood would like to thank Commander John M. Mackay,
Mr John Clark, Mr John H.K. Williamson, Mr J.R. Welsh,
Mr and Mrs Bagg and secretarial staff at 84, PLK John
Boath, PLK and Mrs Magnus Pearson, PLK
and Mrs George Pearson, Captain James W. Hunter,
Mrs Peggy Buchan, and the officers and crew of
MV *Pole Star*.

Photograph on page 1 of the original lighthouse on North
Ronaldsay; on page 3 Duncansby Head Lighthouse; on
page 73 *Pharos* on the annual storing run, at Kyleakin
minor lighthouse.

For additional photographs and illustrations the publishers
would like to thank: The *Glasgow Herald* for the
photographs on pages 8, 10, 55, 63, 66; The National
Portrait Gallery of Scotland for the portraits on pages 11,
20, 30, 31, 44; The Mitchell Library, Glasgow, for the
illustrations on pages 13, 16, 19; The Signal Tower
Museum, Arbroath for the illustrations on pages 22, 23, 24,
25, 29, 32, 38, 65; The Royal Museum of Scotland and
Captain James W. Hunter for the photographs on pages 3,
26, 28, 31, 59; Captain James W. Hunter for the
photographs on pages 42, 47, 51, 60; and Sheriff P.I. Caplan
QC for the top photograph on page 56.

First published 1986
Published by William Collins Sons and Company Limited
© Volume William Collins Sons and Company Limited
© Photographs Keith Allardyce

ISBN 0 00 435660 8

Cartography by Mike Shand
Printed in Great Britain by Blantyre Press
Typeset by John Swain and Son Ltd
Colour origination by Arneg Ltd

CONTENTS

IN THE BEGINNING

Scotland's edge is only here and there rounded off and soft with sand. Mostly, it is an abrupt off-cutting of land in rearing cliffs, with the shelving shore a jumble of broken rock, hidden at high tides. In the seas around is a scattering of almost eight hundred islands — some large and inhabited, some small and colonized by grateful sea birds, some merely vicious little points that mark the summits of hidden reefs, and all stretching the country's boundaries northwards towards the Arctic Circle and far westwards into the Atlantic. These are the regions the earliest geographers called Ultima Thule — the northmost places in the inhabited world, they thought — and round the islands swirl and buffet ocean and sea waters, creating some of the most dangerous tide races and sea storms on earth.

Since unrecorded time, ships coming to battle or to trade have braved these seas, and the Scots, that hardy mix of Celt and Viking, developed a special relationship with the sea. It was their only route to the world beyond, bypassing their 'auld enemy' to the south. And in times of relative peace it was still easier to trade by sea than to cart goods from place to place over uncertain and often unmade roads.

Records of Scottish trade in the Middle Ages demonstrate how negligible a barrier the seas were to the Scots. In the 13th century they had a lively commerce with Bruges, Dieppe and the Baltic port of Lübeck taking fish, wool and hides and bringing home fine cloth, flax and wine. By the middle of the century Dundee, for instance, had become one of the principal wine-importing ports in Europe, creating the kind of wealth that made the burgh a prime target for generations of attack from the sea. Glasgow, too, with its university and cathedral, had a considerable early trade with France, buying wine and selling salmon. The import of claret into Scotland, however, is most closely associated with the growth of the port of Leith in the Firth of Forth. Amongst other imports through Leith in the 15th century were wheat, rye and malt, and Scottish merchants by that time had set themselves up in Lübeck, Stralsund and Danzig on the Baltic and in Veere in Holland, dealing chiefly in wool cloth and salt salmon and herring.

One vital factor in the lucrative salt-fish trade was the availability of coastal salt which was processed in great iron pans over coal fires at various locations along the Forth estuary and on the Angus coast as far north as Montrose. The making of salt had been begun in the 12th century by monks in Lothian, who also first exploited the huge coal deposits there and in Fife. It took the burning of as much as six tons of coal to produce one ton of salt, and since the process took at least twenty-four hours, the fires would have glowed both day and night, providing some guidance into the Firths of Forth and Tay — indeed, the only help at night that mariners could hope for was the flickering light of a beacon on an occasional headland. There is a tradition of a torch beacon on Eilean Glas in the Minch in the 15th century and of a lamp of some sort at Covesea Skerries near Lossiemouth in the Moray Firth. There are early references, too, to beacons on the Angus hills, and on the Isle of May 10th-century monks were said to have kept a beacon burning to guide sea travellers on the pilgrims' way to the holy shrines at St Andrews.

In England as early as the 13th century, there was a seamen's fraternity consisting of 'Godly disposed men who did bind themselves together in the love of Lord Christ in the name of the Masters and Fellow of Trinity Guild, to succour from the dangers of the sea all who are beset upon the coast of England to feed them when ahungered and athirst, to bind up their wounds and to build and light proper beacons for the guidance of mariners.'

Sadly, the earliest records of the activities of the Trinity Brethren were destroyed by fire in 1714. Under the Royal Charter granted in 1514 by Henry VIII, the governing body of Trinity House consisted of one Master, four Wardens and eight Assistants with the power to admit other Brothers and Sisters to the Guild. The Sisters had vanished quite without trace by the time James VI and I came along with his Charter dividing the Brethren into Elder and Younger.

It was in 1565, in the reign of Elizabeth I, that the Corporation of Trinity House were authorized to erect 'beacons, marks and signs of the sea', the principle being to make the sea approaches safer for merchantmen who have 'by the lack of such marks, of late years been miscarried, perished and lost at sea, to the great detriment and hurt of the common weal, and the perishing of no small number of people'. The Act to implement this, however, did not attempt to remove from the Crown the right to grant its own patents to persons who might wish to raise a light and charge dues in return for the payment of rent to the Crown. It was, in fact, to be almost three centuries before Trinity House was given the authority to purchase these lighthouses.

Nevertheless, there was much progress in lighting the English coasts from 1565 onwards. Within 150 years there were 15 lighthouses along the English and Welsh coasts, and five or six round Ireland. No

8

matter that the lights were often furtive and wan, they were a source
of considerable envy and remark by Scottish merchantmen as they
began to trade more freely down the English east coast and through
the Channel in the years after the Union of the Crowns.

THE FIRST LIGHTS

The early 1600s were years of tremendous expansion in Scotland's
trade, and that trade and the problems arising were perpetual topics
for discussion raised at the Convention of Royal Burghs. This meeting
of representatives from all over Scotland came into being in the 16th
century and became an extraordinarily successful pressure group,
surviving to this day as the Convention of Scottish Local Authorities.

In March 1625, Sir James Learmonth of Balcomie, Crail, in the East
Neuk of Fife, stated to the Convention that several of his neighbours
had complained of having sustained losses of both ships and goods
'through lack of a beacon upon the land in Fifeness, and considering
that the House of Balcomie was an convenient place for setting a light
at the said land for preventing of such inconvenience in time coming',
Sir James asked the delegates to take his proposal back to their burghs
for advice and approval and the matter would be raised again at a later
meeting. A few months later, the Convention failed to agree on the
beacon, and Sir James's idea was dropped. But a good notion dies
hard, and for some years to come the matter of lighting the entrance to
the Firth of Forth from various locations was a subject of petition and
strenuous debate. Meanwhile, the river traffic increased steadily, and
with it the incidence of shipwreck and loss of life.

Finally, in 1635, after lengthy collection of evidence on the pros and
cons (an outstanding con being the expense to the merchants of light
dues) a Crown Patent in the English manner was granted to James
Maxwell of Innerwick and John and Alexander Cunningham of Barns,
to build a light on the Isle of May and to levy charges on shipping,
from which charges the King was to be paid £1,000 Scots per annum.
The dues to be paid to Maxwell and the Cunninghams were set at two
shillings Scots per ton for Scottish ships and twice that rate for
foreigners, including English ships, the money to be payable by any
ship coming from or going to beyond an imaginary line from Dunottar
Castle to St Abb's Head.

The Isle of May light is the only feature depicted on the island in the
Blaeu Atlas of Scotland, printed in Holland in 1654. What is shown is a
blazing bright light, which was something the beacon certainly did not
produce with any kind of regularity as it consumed upwards of 200
tons of sometimes wet and inferior coal each year, coal that had to be
hauled up by the lightkeeper, who lived with his family on the island,
to the circular grate on top of the tower that still stands today,
foursquare to the buffeting winds of the river mouth. The May beacon
rarely gave off a satisfactory light and was easily confused with other
fires from salt pans and limekilns on the coast, which is probably why
in the succeeding 150 years only three other private attempts were
made to establish lights of any kind of significance.

At the mouth of the River Tay in 1687, the Fraternity of Masters
and Seamen of Dundee were allowed to erect two lights on Buddon
Ness on the dangerous sandy shallows of the north shore of the
estuary. In due time the Buddon lights were rebuilt and the original

*The lighthouse at Southerness in
Dumfriesshire, built in 1748 by Dumfries
Town Council. It is now a museum.*

coal braziers replaced by a lantern and later by oil lamps fuelled with whale oil. The growing port of Dundee in the Firth of Tay had by that time an important stake in the whaling industry, and whale oil for fuel was becoming plentiful by the end of the 18th century.

By the time the Buddon lights were being fitted with their first lamps, the Union of the Parliaments had ensured once and for all trading rights in the growing British Empire for Scottish merchants. No one south of the border appears to have challenged the fact that the May Isle levy still charged English vessels the foreign rate!

West coast Scots were particularly quick to seize the opportunities now offered of trading with Ireland and the colonies in the New World, and the next lights of any significance were in the west, at Southerness and on Little Cumbrae. The first, at Southerness in Dumfriesshire, was built on a headland marking the river approach to Dumfries, then an important port with a thriving merchant fleet.

In the same era, Glasgow, as a potential port, had very little to commend it. Even shallow-draught boats had difficulty negotiating the narrow muddy little Clyde as far upriver as the small cathedral city. How the silty awkwardness of their river was overcome by dredging and rechannelling thanks to the determination of Glasgow merchants to trade with the New World, is a remarkable story that has relevance here in that in 1743 the shipmasters of Clyde vessels petitioned the Council and Magistrates of Glasgow, demanding the building of lighthouses on the river and at its mouth to make it safer for shipping.

One of several large Clyde estuary obstacles identified in the petition was the island of Little Cumbrae, and in due course a Bill was promoted in Parliament by the City of Glasgow whereby, amongst

The original coal-fired beacon on the Isle of May, the oldest lighthouse in Scotland.

other things, Little Cumbrae lighthouse would be built and the dues
from vessels would be paid not to individuals, as at the May light, nor
to a fraternity of sailors, as at Dundee, but to trustees. The money
would be used exclusively for the upkeep of the light and for the
creation of other lights and markers. Thus, for the first time, an
authority was set up for the principal purpose of lighthouse provision.

The original light on Little Cumbrae was a coal beacon, and
perpetual dissatisfaction with the quality of the light gave a
considerable impetus to research into candle or oil lamps as
alternatives. However, it is not as technological pioneers that the
Clyde Lighthouse Trustees earn their place in history but as the men
who demonstrated how a country's lighthouses could be built and
managed. And that this should now be a matter for serious
consideration increasingly preoccupied Scots in the 18th century, the
second half of which was to become known as their Golden Age.

PRELUDE TO ACT ONE

One great Scot of that era, who was neither philosopher nor preacher,
nor poet nor painter, nor even architect, but a lawyer and practical
forthright politician, was George Dempster of Dunnichen in Angus.
Dempster, who lived from 1732 to 1818 and was the son and grandson
of Dundee merchants, inheriting a large fortune while comparatively
young, devoted much of his lifetime to 'improving' in an age of great
agricultural, social and industrial reform and innovation.

In 1755, after studying at St Andrews and Edinburgh Universities,
Dempster went on the Grand Tour of Europe that was *de rigueur* in
the education of young lairds of the time but which was often
rendered impossible by some European war or other, usually involving
France and Britain, either separately or oppositely. On his return,
Dempster practised at the Bar for a time, made firm friendships with
the Edinburgh luminaries of his time and then, in 1762, was elected as
Member of Parliament for Forfar and Fife Burghs. He was to remain a
member for 28 years, earning for himself the nickname 'Honest
George'.

In an era of political self-servery, Dempster would have none of it.
Instead, he used his position to promote what he considered to be for
the common good. Still a considerable merchant in his native burgh, he
had a vested interest in the formation of the Society for the Extension
and Protection of Fisheries. He actively encouraged the export of fresh
instead of salt salmon from Scottish waters by demonstrating how the
fish could be preserved and packed in ice instead of salt.

We can be sure that Dempster would have been as aware as anyone
of the dangers to life and fortune of sailing round Scotland's shores.
While serving as Provost of the burgh of Forfar in 1784, he attended a
meeting of the Convention of Royal Burghs and introduced for debate
a subject that was in the forefront of everyone's mind.

Two years before, there had been an unprecedented series of storms
around Britain's coasts. There was talk of it being even worse than the
tempests that had wrecked the Spanish Armada in 1588, and more
sustained in violence than the great storm of 1703 in which Henry
Winstanley and his team building the first frail Eddystone Lighthouse
had been washed away. The several surveys of the coasts produced as a
result of the 1782 storms had highlighted the want of lighthouses and

The Little Cumbrae lighthouse in the Clyde estuary.

prompted the Convention to press Parliament to act on the matter of lighthouses in Scotland's most dangerous sea areas. These had been identified in the reports as including the Pentland Firth, the Mull of Kintyre, Scalpay in the Minch, and Kinnaird Head in Aberdeenshire.

At George Dempster's urging, a Commons committee was set up and in a short time had recommended to the House that a Bill be prepared for the setting up of a board of trustees, or Commissioners, with the authority to build lights in the recommended places and to levy dues on every British and foreign ship passing any of the lights. The Bill was presented to the Commons on 31 May 1786. It had been drafted by John Gray, a Writer to the Signet, who was to become the first Secretary of the Northern Lighthouse Board. So well and thorough was the preparation that, with only one slight amendment, the Bill was on the statute books in less than a month.

It must be borne in mind that it was to be almost a century before the Scottish Office came into being and, as a consequence, there was no ready-made official body of civil servants responsible to central ministries to undertake the building of the lighthouses. The Commissioners, therefore, had to be drawn from what had remained to Scotland of her own political structure after the Union of the Parliaments in 1707. Her educational, legal and religious systems had remained intact, and the Convention of Royal Burghs had survived.

It was one of the features of Edinburgh's — and Scotland's — Golden Age that the legal profession made a very important contribution to economic and intellectual developments. Its members also made tidy fortunes, so that by the time the first streets of James Craig's elegant New Town were nearing completion in the late 1780s, nearly two-thirds of all the lawyers in Edinburgh had taken up residence there, cheek by jowl with the aristocracy.

Not surprisingly, then, the Northern Lighthouse Board was born with a built-in bias towards members of the legal profession, but with the likely leavening of a group of burgh provosts and baillies. Heading the list of proposed Trustees of the Board were Scotland's two Crown officers, the Lord Advocate and the Solicitor General. Next came the Lord Provosts and senior baillies of Edinburgh and Glasgow, and the Provosts of Aberdeen, Inverness and Campbeltown. To these representatives of a very restricted electorate were added the Sheriffs of Edinburgh, Lanark, Renfrew, Bute, Argyll, Inverness, Ross, Orkney, Caithness and Aberdeen.

In 1786, the American War of Independence had been over for three years; Edmund Cartwright's power loom was transforming weaving technology; Matthew Boulton declared people were going steam-engine mad; the pace of production in both the linen and cotton industries was leading to unprecedented expansion and export opportunities. On the River Carron at Falkirk, the great iron works had been in production for over twenty years. Boulton and Watt's steam engine was demanding coal supplies as never before; all over Scotland new seams were opened, and the only practical means of moving the new generation of goods and raw materials was by river and sea. There was no time to be lost in confronting the long-vexed problem of making Scotland's sea roads safer for mariners.

On 1 August 1786, the Commissioners of the Northern Lighthouse Board assembled for the first time to begin their appointed task of building lighthouses at Kinnaird Head, North Ronaldsay, Eilean Glas and the Mull of Kintyre.

George Dempster of Dunnichen (1732-1818) by J. T. Nairn.

THE FIRST STEPS

According to the minutes of the first meeting of the Commissioners, held in Edinburgh 'in the twenty-sixth year of the Reign of his present Majesty', those attending were: Sir James Hunter-Blair, Bart, Lord Provost of the City of Edinburgh; James Dickson, Esq., eldest Baillie of Edinburgh; Robert Dundas, Esq., Solicitor General for Scotland; Ballantyne William McLeod, Esq., Sheriff Depute of Bute; William Honeyman, Esq., Sheriff Depute of Lanark; and Alexander Elphinston, Esq., Sheriff Depute of Aberdeen. They elected the Lord Provost of Edinburgh their Preses, and John Gray, Writer to the Signet — he who had so efficiently drawn up the founding Bill — was nominated to be 'clerk during the pleasure of the Trustees' and remained as Secretary until he retired in 1811.

No time was wasted in getting down to the business in hand. It was announced that in July Edinburgh Town Council had guaranteed the Lord Provost and the eldest Baillie, along with the other four burghs, of any sum not exceeding a total of £1,200, this being the amount they were allowed to borrow under the Act.

The Act had also laid down the scale of charges to be made to shipping *once all four lights had been built.* The dues were originally fixed at one penny (just under ½p) per ton on British ships and two pennies (just under 1p) per ton on foreign vessels passing any of the lights, either leaving or arriving at British ports or passing the coast on passage for elsewhere or engaging in coastal trade. Exemptions from these payments were granted to whaling fleets and to those ships making the Archangel and White Sea run.

Since receiving his copy of the Act, Sir James Hunter-Blair had taken the opportunity to discuss the subject with the other Trustees who had attended the Convention of Royal Burghs where the matter had been long discussed, and he had already written to several people who might be able to assist the Board by advising on how best they could set about putting up the four lighthouses. A reply had already been received from a gentleman in Liverpool, and this letter had been accompanied by a chart of Liverpool harbour and four lighthouses 'with answers to a variety of Queries, two years account of the expence [sic], Regulations for the harbour and docks with a printed book on sailing and the construction of Lighthouses with lamps and reflectors'. The volume of the reply begs imagining the number of questions that must have been in the letter that inspired it! And the correspondent of Liverpool was not the only person to have been approached. Sir James had also, he announced, received a plan of the lighthouse on the Isle of May and, from the Provost of Dundee, an elevation plan of the Buddon lights on the Tay and an estimate of what the building costs had been.

It was a good start to the vital collection of information, and a committee was formed to proceed with the collation of information, 'preparing matters for general meetings and for carrying into execution such particulars as may be remitted to them'. Three was to be enough to form a quorum, and Lord Provost Hunter-Blair was to be convener of the small committee. But perhaps the most significant announcement the Lord Provost had to make on that August day was 'that he had received from Thomas Smith, tinplate worker in Edinburgh, observations on Lighthouses by Reflectors with a small model'.

Minutes of the first meeting of the Commissioners, 1 August 1986.

Fraserburgh, aquatint by William Daniell.

THE FIRST ENGINEER

Thomas Smith, son of a Dundee ship's captain, was born at Broughty
Ferry near Dundee in the 1750s. On the premature death of his father,
Thomas was raised by his mother, the daughter of a Leith shipmaster
and owner, and was apprenticed to a Dundee tinsmith, although he
had always longed to go to sea, like his father and grandfather before
him.

By 1764, when young Thomas began his apprenticeship, Dundee
had begun to develop its whaling fleet, and the ready supply of whale
oil in the town had led to Dundonians abandoning tallow candles for
oil lamps — usually a simple wick set to burn above a small reservoir of
oil. This produced an inconstant, smelly and usually smoky light. The
making of oil lamps formed a significant part of any metalworker's
business in the second half of the 18th century, and it was doubtless
when Thomas Smith was learning his craft that the question of good
lights began to intrigue him. His father had been a member of the
Fraternity of Seamen who had built the Buddon lights, and the young
Smith was well aware of the shortcomings of these lights and the
terrible dangers to sailors in Scotland's coastal waters.

His apprenticeship served, Thomas Smith moved to Edinburgh to
live with his mother's family, and in a very few years was in business
making oil lamps. He prospered. He married. He became consultant
manufacturer of street lamps to Edinburgh Town Council. He might
have been content simply to develop his excellent business. But there
was a certain restlessness about him, betraying perhaps the heart of a

frustrated merchant sailor but which manifested itself in endless experimentation with lights, to improve them, to brighten them.

In Geneva, around 1784, a lamp which was to revolutionize oil lighting was constructed by Aimé Argand. It had a circular wick, by which means Argand found he could better control the consumption of oil, and a glass chimney which had the twin effect of controlling the draught to the light and making it burn several times brighter.

Thomas Smith had constructed a lamp with a parabolic reflector in an attempt to enhance its luminosity, and to this he now added Argand's glass chimney. This was no doubt the lamp the model of which he had sent to that first meeting of the Commissioners. The actual lamp was set up on the island of Inchkeith in the River Forth, and it proved immediately that this method of lighting was infinitely preferable to that uncertain flickering smoky beacon on the May.

On 1 September 1786 the small committee of the Trustees met. Sir James Hunter-Blair, James Dickson and Sheriffs Elphinston and Honeyman heard that Mr John Traill, owner of the island of North Ronaldsay in the Orkneys, had written 'requesting free acceptance of the ground necessary for erecting the lighthouse in any part of his property'. The three other landowners involved in the plans — the Duke of Argyll for the Mull of Kintyre, Macleod of Harris for Eilean Glas and Lord Saltoun for Kinnaird Head where there was already a castle tower on which a light could be erected — were rather more dilatory in their response to the Trustees, and in Lord Saltoun's case the Commissioners eventually had to threaten to use their powers of compulsory purchase.

Two other significant matters were dealt with at that September meeting. First, advertisements had been placed in all newspapers and journals, seeking building estimates for the four lighthouses. No one had replied. Secondly, a letter had been received from the Glasgow Chamberlain about the lights on Little Cumbrae and enclosed was a copy of a letter from Glasgow's Dean of Guild about lighthouses in New England and Liverpool, amongst other places. The Dean of Guild had also given his opinions on the proper height and size of lighthouses.

To the reader two hundred years on, the overwhelming impression gleaned from the minutes of these first meetings is of an almost touching ingenuousness. Public figures of their era, these Trustees had been given a highly significant job to do, constructing lighthouses in some of the wildest, stormiest places on the globe. They were amply demonstrating the will to get down to it, but they had very soon discovered that they seriously lacked the means. The technology they urgently needed for Scotland's particular conditions had simply not been developed, and one wonders if they would have gone at the work with such a will had they realized that the development of lighthouse technology was to be largely the work of their own engineers in the years to come.

In September 1786 they were still utterly unsure of how it was all to begin and yet positive that it had to. The raising of loans, the acquisition of the lighthouse sites, long letters of questions and advice, these were part and parcel of the kind of work which was familiar to them all. But what kind of lighthouses would it be best to build? Of that they had absolutely no idea and desperately needed to find someone who might know. One Ezekiel Walker of King's Lynn in Norfolk was highly recommended to them, and the committee were informed that a letter had been sent to him to ask if he could advise them on what to do, or maybe undertake the building of the lights or at least oversee their execution.

By the General Meeting held in January 1787 still no one had replied to the advertisement for building tenders, which was not surprising since neither specification nor design of building had been forthcoming from the Commissioners. But there had been progress of a kind on other fronts. Lord Saltoun had written with a plan of the elevation of the Tower Castle on the ground at Kinnaird Head, demanding an inflated price for the property. In Orkney, the search was on for building materials for the North Ronaldsay light, once a suitable plan for it had been found.

It was decided that everyone concerned with the projects would be circularized with the information on the construction and height of lighthouses just as soon as Mr Ezekiel Walker produced such a thing. Mr Walker had been in constant correspondence with the Board since September and had provided a description of the efficacy of lights with reflectors and an estimate of the annual expense of their upkeep. He had also indicated his willingness to come north, build one lighthouse himself and advise on the building of the other three, 'or for 50 guineas would instruct any one person the Trustees thought proper to send in the whole of his principles and improvements'. That willingness of Walker's to share his knowledge so openly is an early example of what was soon to become general practice amongst lighthouse engineers and lamp technicians. Information on improved methods derived from experience has always been exchanged.

The person the Trustees thought proper to send was Thomas Smith who had, it was recorded in the minutes, already made proposals for lighting with lamps and reflectors and experimented and laid models before the Trustees, 'which on account of his want of experience had not hitherto been agreed to'. On the other hand, with the shrewdness and canniness that marks their management, the Trustees had evidently been impressed enough to decide that once Smith were instructed they would be able to dispense perhaps with Walker's services. Mr Walker was informed that Thomas Smith would be sent to King's Lynn and that the 50 guineas would be forthcoming after Smith was fully instructed. Thomas was given £15 for expenses and sent on his way.

THE FIRST FOUR LIGHTS

Thomas was back in Edinburgh in a matter of weeks, since it was reported to the Board on 21 March that he was now instructed. An Edinburgh architect called Kay, perhaps a relative of Smith's since Kay was his mother's maiden name, was asked to make drawings of the four proposed lighthouses, and as soon as Smith, still with Walker's guidance, had approved their design, their height and position, and so on, the plans were sent to all concerned.

Thomas Smith was sent to the Carron Ironworks to procure an estimate for the cast iron to be used in the construction of the lamps. Such was the progress at Carron that their cast product was now much cheaper than the beaten iron produced by traditional smiths. From Carron he went to Glasgow to buy mirror glass for his reflectors, again more cheaply than it could be purchased elsewhere.

16

The Start Point Lighthouse on Sanday, Orkney, an aquatint by William Daniell.

The lights were underway at last. At least the first light, at Kinnaird Head, was, and it was devoutly hoped by the Commissioners that the other three would follow very quickly. Since there was no other potential source of revenue than the light dues, it was imperative that all the lights be completed, and it was becoming increasingly evident that the original limit on the Board's borrowings was seriously below the likely expenditure. What they had paid for the Kinnaird Head site and its castle tower was already half as much again as the original £1,200, and by early 1788 around £4,000 of debts had been amassed. For a time it looked as though the entire venture might founder, but a further Act of Parliament in that year allowed the Board to begin charging half their light dues as soon as they had two out of the four lights ready. In fact, given the utter lack of experience of all concerned in the enterprise, the Kinnaird Head light was completed and lit in a remarkably short space of time.

Since no one had ventured to reply to the renewed advertisements for a contractor to undertake the building, the Board asked Thomas Smith to assume that role as well as that of designer and light builder. It was just another problem to add to those he was already coping with, and not least of these was the design of the new lights and their reflectors. It had soon become clear to Thomas that there was to be no 'mass' production of lights. The four chosen sites each demanded that the lighthouses and the lights they contained be at different elevations and be visible from various distances. In the end each lighthouse had to have its own custom-built light. In addition to his work on the lights and his supervision of the conversion of the Kinnaird Head castle tower into a lighthouse, Smith was also sent off to inspect and finally select the sites for the other three lighthouses.

Thomas Smith excites profound admiration in anyone who stops to consider the timetable of work he undertook in that first year of the Board's existence. Here was a family man with a considerable business of his own to attend to in Edinburgh, living in an age of literal horse-power for overland transport, while at sea the traveller was entirely at the mercy of winds and tides and nowhere more so than in the dangerous waters Smith's work was hoped to render a little safer.

At Kinnaird Head, despite all the inherent problems of the site and the necessity to anchor a boat off-shore as a kind of floating stores depot to ensure that there was as little delay as possible in getting building supplies on site, by the end of November 1787 the lamp had been shipped from Edinburgh and installed.

Smith's next job at the Board's behest was to recruit the lighthouse staff. James Park, a retired sea captain, was employed at a wage of one shilling (5p) per night plus free lodging, 'on condition that he has another person with him every night who he is to instruct in the manner of cleaning the lantern and cleaning and lighting the lamps'. In addition to his wage and shelter, James Park was also provided with pasturage for one cow.

In one fell swoop the Commissioners had created not only the job of lightkeeper but realized he needed an assistant lightkeeper to help him perform what was — and remains — the prime object of the service, to provide a bright shining light, although it was not until 1815 that Assistant Lightkeepers were actually formally appointed by the Board. It must be assumed, therefore, that among the original assistants were wives and children of lightkeepers.

And so all was set. Notices were placed in the *London Gazette* and in Scottish newspapers, informing sailors of the whereabouts of the new light and describing how it would appear to them from 1 December 1787. Sixteen months to the day from that first General Meeting of the Commissioners they had their first lighthouse and their first lighthouse keeper. They also had their first site engineer, their first lamp technician, their first personnel officer, their first superintendent of lights, and their first building contractor. That these last were all the same man must count as the finest return the Board ever had from an outlay of 50 guineas in its two hundred years' history!

When the Kinnaird Head light was lit, the Commissioners took no time for celebration. The urgent need to complete the second light and so begin to earn some revenue was the foremost thought in the Board's mind.

Thomas Smith was already aware of the contrast between the Kinnaird Head site and the three others. Kinnaird Head lies close to the fishing town of Fraserburgh where there was not only a ready supply of men to carry out the building work but the building materials were also at hand. The Mull of Kintyre, on the other hand, is the cliff-blunt tip of a finger of land that juts southwards into the North Channel and is within sight of the north of Ireland. Even today there is a mere track across miles of rough hilly moorland from the village of Southend to the 250-foot-high cliffs on which the lighthouse was built. A sea approach suitable for bringing building materials to the site was impossible for the very cliff hazard the light was set to signal.

Every single item for the building of the light on the Mull of Kintyre had to be carted in small bulk by packhorse from the base at Campbeltown, twelve miles distant. Despite this, by April 1788 the tower was ready for the installation of the light. There was some delay while Thomas Smith, in his role as personnel officer, tried to ensure that this bleak isolated headland would provide a slightly more tolerable existence than the original plans appeared to provide. He insisted, for instance, that a wall be built between the lighthouse and the sea 'to prevent the keeper or any of his family from being blown over by the strong winds'. Matthew Hardie, a local crofter, was recruited at £50 per annum as the light's first keeper, and as soon as Thomas Smith had satisfied himself that all was in order, the light was lit for the first time in October 1788.

Now that there were two up and two to go, the Board were impatient to complete their task. The North Ronaldsay and Scalpay lights were in progress, but the progress was painfully slow. The building of the North Ronaldsay light had been undertaken by local contractors working to a plan for a tower sixty feet in height with an adjacent house for the lightkeeper. Although the building had gone on well in the summer of 1788, when the winter closed in there was still much to do. Meanwhile, from Scalpay there had come a report that the tenant of the ground which had been proposed for the lighthouse had determined to make a start on a lighthouse of his own devising. It isn't clear whether he thought he was going to be able to claim dues from passing ships, but the Commissioners quickly despatched Thomas Smith and an Edinburgh mason called George Mills, whom they had appointed to build the light, to find out precisely what was going on.

Smith and Mills finally got to Scalpay in the early summer of 1788 by a devious and strenuous journey, and at the site at Eilean Glas they found seven feet of tower already built — but four feet wider than the original plan, of which the tenant had apparently acquired a copy. What to do? There was no easy way in which the two Edinburgh men could return for instructions. The practical Smith decided that it would be best simply to accommodate the additional width into the design and for Mills to remain at Eilean Glas to supervise the structure and to keep a very careful note of the day to day expenses incurred. In the autumn Smith reported to the Commissioners that although the work on both the lighthouse and the keeper's accommodation was completed, they were already being lashed by heavy seas.

The following year, the Commissioners hired a boat to take the lights and the lighthouse-keepers' families to North Ronaldsay and to Eilean Glas, and on 1 October 1789 — just a little over three years from the first meeting of the Commissioners — the job which they had been assembled to do had been completed, and the four lights were the object of immediate universal praise from Scottish and foreign mariners.

EXTENDING POWERS

Indeed, so impressive were the lights that now requests came in from several quarters for additional lighthouses. A further Act of Parliament, passed in 1789, enabled the Commissioners 'to cause such other lighthouses to be erected upon any parts of the coast of Scotland as they shall deem necessary'. In the same Act they were also given the

right 'when any new lighthouse shall be erected on any part of the coast of Scotland . . . to elect the Provost or Chief Magistrate of the nearest Royal Burgh, and also the Sheriff Depute of the nearest county to the said new-erected lighthouse, to be Commissioners'.

A 'Memorial of State', presented to the Board on 12 July 1803, details the achievements to that date. After the first four lights, the Board had then built a lighthouse on Pladda, a small island off the south end of the Isle of Arran in the Firth of Clyde, and first lit in 1790. There followed two lights on the Pentland Skerries, both first lit on 1 October 1794, the northmost 116 feet high and the other $94\frac{1}{2}$ feet above high water. On Start Point, the eastern tip of the Orkney island of Sanday, a beacon tower was being converted to hold what was to be the Commissioners' first revolving light, and on the island of Inchkeith in the Firth of Forth, a new lighthouse was under construction.

So much progress had been made in light building that the Board was out of the financial wood and confidently forecasting a time when surplus revenues would accrue as much interest as to make the lights and the building of lights self-funding. Meantime, exemption from paying dues continued to be given to Royal Navy ships and to whalers and those trading with Archangel, 'provided the said ships return before the 15th of September each year'. British ships were charged

The Mull of Kintyre sketched in 1848 by John Christian Schetky.

$1\frac{1}{2}$ pennies (just over $\frac{1}{2}$p) per ton for passing any or all of the lighthouses, while foreign vessels paid three pennies ($1\frac{1}{2}$p).

The Trustees of the Clyde Lights, which had been formed to build the Little Cumbrae light fifty years before, had also come under considerable pressure to provide more lights in the upper Clyde. The Glasgow merchants had continued dredging and realigning their river. Seagoing ships were now able to sail right up to the warehouses and wharves in the heart of what was to become the second greatest city of the British Empire. A lighthouse with a lamp by Thomas Smith replaced the coal brazier on Little Cumbrae, and a new lighthouse had also been built at Cloch Point, just where the Clyde estuary turns eastwards to Glasgow.

On the east coast, demands for lights continued, as did the increasing use of the northern route to the Atlantic. The southern North Sea and Channel waters were dangerous places now that Britain was once again involved in wars, this time with post-Revolutionary France, eager to stake her claims to empire. Patrolling French ships and Royal Navy press gangs were the bane of the Lighthouse Board's life for many of the early years of its activities.

The wild outlying places in which its own empire was growing were always going to prove difficult to get to, but as early as the 1790s Thomas Smith was making regular annual tours of inspection, and stores were being delivered by a specially chartered ship of 100 tons. These tours undertaken by Smith, not to mention his other work with lamps and lightkeepers on behalf of the Board, were so time-consuming and pressing that around 1790 he began to look around for an apprentice. The 19-year-old son of a widow, who had long been a friend of the Smith family, was invited to join the firm as an apprentice lamp engineer.

The young man had been at one time destined for the ministry. A contemporary and friend of Walter Scott, he had attended the Royal High School in Edinburgh, but childhood visits to the Smith workshop had kindled in him an enthusiasm for things mechanical, and so it was that Scotland lost a potential preacher but gained one of her finest innovative engineers — Robert Stevenson.

From the very beginning of his career, Stevenson worked closely with Thomas Smith on lighthouse projects. Their professional closeness became a family bond when in 1792 the twice-widowed Smith married Robert's widowed mother, Jean. And then, in 1799, the family tie was made closer still when Robert Stevenson married Thomas' daughter, Jane.

Robert Stevenson soon found himself being given more and more responsibility on the lighthouse side of Smith's business, and in due course he was undertaking the lighthouse inspection tours on his own, calculating the oil stores, adjusting the lights, attending to the needs of the keepers and their families, surveying sites for new lights. Gradually Smith withdrew from the strenuous job he had created and for which he had set the style and standard. His attention to detail, his sincere caring for the wellbeing of the small band of keepers and their families living in inhospitable inaccessible places, his skill as a lampmaker ever on the outlook for improvements that would make the light brighter and more sure, these were Thomas Smith's most enduring bequests to the Commissioners and the service in their charge. He also spared them the considerable bother of finding and training his successor as Engineer of Northern Lighthouses. The job passed to Robert Stevenson.

Robert Stevenson (1772-1850) by John Syme.

THE BELL ROCK

Poet Laureate Robert Southey's tale of how Ralph the Rover cuts down the warning bell and then founders on the rock used to be every child's introduction to the story of this dangerous reef just off the east coast. Lying twelve miles off Arbroath on the Angus coast — the Aberbrothok of the poem — this legendary hazard to shipping is a long ridge, only partly revealing itself above water at the lowest of tides. The waters around the reef are deceptively deeper than the surrounding sea bottom so that mariners making soundings in the days before the lighthouse was built would find themselves in deep water, think themselves clear of the danger then steer straight on to the reef lurking just below.

On 17 January 1793, Admiral Alexander Inglis Cochrane, on board *HMS Hind* anchored in Leith Roads, sat down to compose a letter to the Commissioners: 'Gentlemen, I think it is a duty I owe to the public to call your attention as Trustees for the Northern Lights, to the great hazard and peril that the trade of the East of Scotland is subject to for want of a lighthouse being created on the Bell or Cape Rock, and the only dangerous one upon this coast from the Staples to Duncansby Head, except the Carr which lies so close to Fifeness and the Isle of May as to render it of little consequence.' From a sailor's viewpoint the rock, continued the Admiral, 'is in the most dangerous situation possible for the trade of the Firths of Forth and Tay, the more so from the prevailing winds on the Coast being from WNW to SW.' And then to demonstrate his knowledge of and interest in lights, he points out the necessity of having the light on the Bell Rock distinguishable from the Isle of May light 'such as is adopted at Scilly and the Caskett, the lights on which revolve, I believe, once in a minute so as to be obscured and visible alternately'.

The Commissioners were well aware of the problem of identification and were working on it. But what kind of structure could possibly withstand the seas and storms at the Bell, if ever a light could be built there? The Admiral had his own idea: the structure would have to be a pillar of stone or iron, with his own personal preference being for iron, which he suggested would offer the least resistance to the seas. And what about getting men on to the rock to build a light? 'The Cape Rock,' the Admiral observed, 'is dry at half tide in common tides and at low water in spring tides is about seven feet out of water for nearly half a mile.'

The Admiral's letter was not the first nor the last appeal for some kind of warning at the Bell Rock. No one knows how many hundreds of sailors down the centuries had lost their lives on the reef or had been driven on to rocks on shore in their efforts to avoid it.

In 1799 the Trustees were forced to grasp the nettle after a series of violent storms in which around seventy vessels were lost along the east coast between St Abb's Head and Duncansby Head. No one was ever certain precisely how many vessels were lost — foreign ships as well as British had vanished without trace in the devastating darkness.

Robert Stevenson was thereupon asked to survey the rock as a matter of urgency, and with considerable difficulty he was finally able to set foot on the Bell Rock on 5 October 1800 to make his measurements and survey the rock. On 22 December he made his report to the Commissioners. The graphic literary style of it was an enduring Stevenson trait. He is not content simply to report on the

The worthy Abbot of Aberbrothok
Had placed that bell on the Inchcape Rock;
On a buoy in the storm it floated and swung,
And over the waves its warning rung.

When the rock was hid by the surge's swell,
The mariners heard the warning bell;
And then they knew the perilous rock,
And blest the Abbot of Aberbrothok.

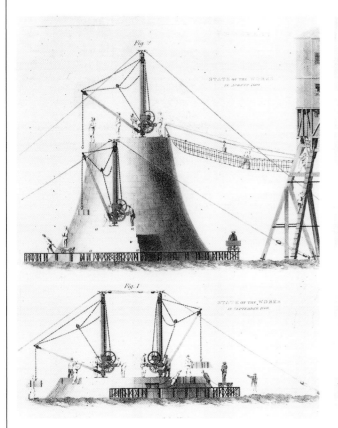

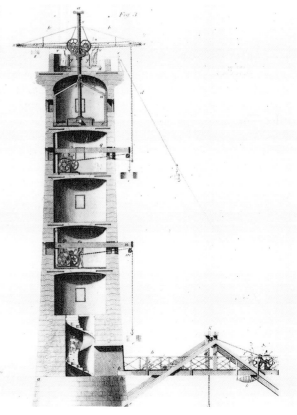

rock but contributes his own picture of the growing commercial scene which makes the building of the light a more pressing matter than ever. The preamble begins:

'During the reign of his present Majesty, the spirit of discovery and improvement in maritime affairs has been conducted with the greatest energy and crowned with such success as can only be equalled by the happy effects that have followed to a nation which, without commerce, must have moved in a sphere perhaps below mediocrity. In proportion therefore as Commerce and Industry are considered essential to the wealth and happiness of the community, every effort to assist the mariner in his course through the pathless ocean, will be regarded both as the call of interest and humanity.

'And doubtless, one of the most prominent causes of that perfection to which navigation has been brought may be ascribed to the accuracy of our sea charts and to an increase of landmarks by which the mariner after braving the dangers of the seas is enabled to guide his ship with safety into her intended port.'

Referring at length to the era before the first Act, he reminds the Commissioners of how shipping had to make a wide sweep round the north of Scotland and over to the west and the Atlantic in order to avoid the terrible dangers of the coast, these mariners being left to 'grope their way from the Firth of Forth to the Firth of Clyde'. As for the Bell Rock, even with all the hazards the rugged Scottish coastline presented, 'I will venture to say there is not a more dangerous situation upon the whole coasts of the Kingdom, or none that calls more loudly to be done than the Cape or Bell Rock'.

Stevenson, then, was as convinced as any that the job ought to be

'State of the works in 1808, 1809 and 1810' of the Bell Rock Lighthouse from Robert Stevenson's An Account of the Bell Rock Lighthouse.

done. But having been on the rock and surveyed it, although he knew it could bear a heavy stone tower such as that built by Smeaton on the Eddystone Rock, the logistics of building such a tower, on a reef that was underwater for the best part of the day and night, almost beggared the imagination. Men and materials would have to be shipped to the site and housed there in some way. The precision required of masons cutting the interlocking stones would be of an unprecedentedly high order. The day to day uncertainties of the North Sea, the fact that three hours would have to be thought of as a good tide's worth of work, the inherent dangers of working on the rugged slippery surface, all made this venture quite unlike any lighthouse building previously undertaken, even the Eddystone. Little wonder Robert Stevenson wrote later, 'I am sure no one was fonder of his own work than I was, till I saw the Bell Rock'.

The Commissioners, too, had problems, financial problems. The estimated cost of £42,000 was far and away beyond their means, and it was necessary to ask Parliament once more for the authority to raise a further loan and impose a special Bell Rock duty on shipping. In due course a Bill was passed, allowing them to borrow £25,000 which, when added to the £20,000 of surplus light duties they had accrued, was sufficient to allow them to proceed.

John Rennie, the grand old man of Scottish civil engineering, was, naturally, consulted about Stevenson's projected design, and he agreed that a stone tower akin to Smeaton's Eddystone would be best suited to the purpose. An 82-ton fishing vessel was converted into a floating light-cum-store and dormitory ship, renamed the *Pharos* and moored about two miles from the rock in July 1807, and the work began of digging out the foundation in the bedrock. By day, sometimes in very rough conditions, by night with torchlight, even on Sundays, the work went on, the devoutly religious Stevenson mollifying his conscience over the Sunday work with the honest thought that building this lighthouse was a Christian activity, destined surely as it was to save lives.

Towards the end of that first October, the work stopped for the season, but before the workmen left the site, they constructed a fifty-foot-high beacon on spidery iron legs, and this structure eventually became a barracks for the builders, relieving them from the often wretched business of being rowed back to the *Pharos* when the tide stopped work.

During the winter of 1807/8, a stone yard and barracks was properly established at Arbroath for the artificers. Aberdeen granite and freestone from the Mylnefield Quarry near Dundee were shipped in, and the masons set to work shaping the blocks which would have to lock together perfectly and three-dimensionally once they had been ferried out to the rock. It is a remarkable fact that not one of these hundreds of stones had to be rejected or altered on the rock.

How the stones, once cut and assembled in their correct order on shore, were to be transported to the site was another vast problem to which Stevenson had to apply himself. It must be remembered that all he had at his disposal were men, boats, muscle and wind power. Two tenders for ferrying the stones were acquired by the Board, the *Smeaton* and the *Sir Joseph Banks*. The stones at Arbroath had to be carefully loaded on to the tenders and as carefully manoeuvred off again at the landing sites on the Bell Rock, then hauled across the reef to the site. The last part of the process was made somewhat easier after

The pattern to which the dovetailed stones for the Bell Rock lighthouse were cut and, above, how they slotted together, from Robert Stevenson's Account.

Stevenson had devised and laid a little rail track. He even installed a forge on the rock to save as much precious time as possible.

In the building season of 1808, only twenty-two working days were possible, but the foundation stone was laid on 10 July of that year, and by the end of September, when work had to be abandoned for the year, the base of the lighthouse was four courses high.

When the workers returned to the rock in April 1809, they found everything intact, and in that year the rate of progress was speeded up considerably when the beacon tower became a barracks. A contemporary observer wrote, 'To the erection of this beacon, the rapidity with which the lighthouse was got up is chiefly to be ascribed: and it is extremely doubtful if ever it would have been accomplished without some such expedient, — certainly not without the loss of many lives; for in a work of this nature, continued for a series of years, it is wonderful that only one life was lost on the rock, by a fall from a rope ladder when the sea ran high, and another at the mooring buoys, by the upsetting of a boat.'

By September, when work had to be given up for another year, the lighthouse was over thirty feet high and well above the high-water mark. At the start of work in 1810 there seemed little likelihood that it would be completed in that year, but by the beginning of August the last part of the stone structure was positioned, and the iron lightroom and light were rapidly installed.

As the men who built that light left the rock for the last time, they may well have expressed great relief that it was all over. They must also have known that for the rest of their lives they would remember the years on the rock, the shared terrors of storms when the lightship broke from her moorings and wallowed helplessly until taken in tow.

Chart of the Inchcape reef with the routes into the lighthouse, from Robert Stevenson's An Account of the Bell Rock Lighthouse.

And those who were there would surely always recall the terrible day that one of the rowing boats that took men off the rock in rising tides was washed away, leaving Robert Stevenson and over thirty men with boats enough for twenty or so, with no hope of signalling for help in the rising storm, until suddenly the appearance of the mail boat from Arbroath had saved the day, and the men. And who was to forget the procession of the last stone for the lighthouse as it was taken to the tender through cheering crowds? And would Robert Stevenson ever forget the energy and time he had expended persuading the press gangs to release his expert workers snatched for His Majesty's service while on off-duty shore leave? Special tokens had been issued to the Bell Rock building team, giving them exemption from military and naval service while the lighthouse was being built — a simple system apparently poorly understood by the gangs.

It had long been said that even if the Bell Rock Lighthouse were built, nobody would be found hardy enough to live in it, yet there was a rush of applicants for the job. However, the man chosen as the first Principal Keeper on the Bell Rock was Captain John Reid who had been acting master and principal lightkeeper of the floating light on the *Pharos*. Since it had been decided that there must always be three keepers on the Bell Rock, assistants were also found for Reid, including men who had been involved in the building.

The new Bell Rock light was an oil lamp with Argand burners with silver-plated reflectors in a parabolic curve. The reflectors were mounted on a frame turning through one revolution every three minutes. Included, too, were shades of red glass so that there was an alternate white and red beam. It was soon reported that in good visibility the beam could be seen twenty-five miles away. Two large bells to give fog signals could be tolled by the same machinery which revolved the light.

John Forrest, the superintendent of lightkeepers, went out to the rock to train the group of keepers in their job, and on 1 February 1811 the Bell Rock light came into service, almost five years after it had been begun, despite the dire dangers of the site, the infuriating attentions of the press gangs, the long and continuing war with Napoleon Bonaparte, and a final cost of building that was almost £20,000 more than the original estimate.

Two years later, it was observed in an agricultural survey of Forfarshire, 'It must be a matter of very general satisfaction to learn that the lighthouse has sustained no injury whatever from the storms of the first and second winters ... Mr Forrest, the Superintendent for the instruction of the light-keepers, after remaining at the lighthouse from December 1810 till April 1811, reported that "the lighthouse was as dry and comfortable as any house in Edinburgh."'

Over 175 years later, Robert Stevenson's Bell Rock Lighthouse still stands monument to his ingenuity, his patience, his attention to detail and his ability to lead men. This great achievement, however, also had the curious effect of rendering the building of other lighthouses a commonplace in the public mind, so that when subsequent great rock challenges were met, these never quite caught the imagination of the ordinary man and woman in the street in the way the building of the Bell Rock Light had done.

Even today, Robert Stevenson's success still tends to overshadow the contribution his successors made. The Stevenson family provided the Northern Lighthouse Board with Engineers for over 130 years, and

The completed Bell Rock Lighthouse from Robert Stevenson's Account.

Chicken Rock Lighthouse, Isle of Man.

in each generation there were challenges met and overcome. Not only did they build rock lighthouses and shore lights in some of the most inaccessible and difficult locations round our shores, but they were tireless innovators and developers in civil engineering and lamp technology. It is in no short measure due to this extraordinarily gifted family that in their first hundred years the Commissioners of Northern Lighthouses built no fewer than 72 lighthouses in Scotland and on the Isle of Man, many of them overcoming incredible difficulties in a manner that would have left even the bold Robert deep in admiration.

Doubtless encouraged by the success of the Bell Rock enterprise, Parliament passed an Act in 1814 giving the Commissioners of Northern Lighthouses the right to take over the old Isle of May light, which had remained in private hands until then, and to replace the unreliable coal beacon with an oil light. It also gave the Board the right to construct further lighthouses, among them those at the Mull of Galloway, Skerryvore, Cape Wrath, Tarbat Ness and Sumburgh Head. Several of these sites had been previously surveyed by Robert Stevenson, and one by one the lights went up until by the 1830s only Skerryvore was left to be tackled.

In 1837, Robert's son Alan was appointed engineer for the construction of the lighthouse on Skerryvore, and after meticulous planning, surveying and designing, work was finally begun in June 1838. A base was set up at Hynish on Tiree, and the stone prepared there was to be transshipped to the rock, twelve miles away to the west, when building operations began. As at the Bell Rock, a boat was to be anchored just off the reef to accommodate the men and stores, and a beacon-cum-barracks was then to be built on Skerryvore, to be occupied by the men and facilitate the work.

Unlike the Bell Rock, Skerryvore was a difficult rock to excavate. There was no flat surface anywhere, just a series of jagged jutting points, and it was into these the men had at first to try to build the beacon. Progress was agonisingly slow, and what little had been achieved was quickly disposed of in a terrible storm. When the winds and seas died down again, there was left only a mere trace or two of a year's work. But in 1839 work began once more, and this time gunpowder was used to help break up the rock. The foundations made progress, slow and hard though it was. Miraculously, despite the use of gunpowder on this tiny fist of rock with no possibility of shelter, only one man was hurt in the operation.

The foundation stone of the actual lighthouse was finally laid, by the Duke of Argyll, in July 1840, and over the next two summers the massive and elegantly curved lighthouse took shape. In September 1843 it was ready with its light for testing. It was a quite wonderful light, the observers reported from the shore station twelve miles away at Hynish. At Skerryvore on 1 February 1844, the light was at last ready to shine out each night, and its power from atop the 158-foot tower was acclaimed a modern wonder. By the time Skerryvore was lit, Alan Stevenson had become Robert's successor as Engineer to the Board.

THE ISLE OF MAN

As early as 1801, Robert Stevenson had reported to the Commissioners that there was a need for a light on the Calf of Man, the southernmost tip of the island which sits athwart several vital western shipping lanes.

Neither the Commissioners of Northern Lighthouses nor Trinity House had rights to build lights on Man in their remit, and it was not until the 1815 Act that the Commissioners were granted permission to erect two lights on the island — one at the Calf of Man and another at the northern tip, the Point of Ayre. It was not, however, until 1854 that an Act was passed giving the Commissioners the general power of erection of lighthouses, beacons and so on in the Isle of Man.

In all, five major lighthouses were built by the Commissioners in the Isle of Man between 1818 and 1880. The Point of Ayre and Calf of Man lights were completed in 1818, and the first Douglas Head light in 1832, all under Robert Stevenson's supervision. His sons, David and Thomas, were responsible in 1859 for redesigning Douglas Head and for building the Chicken Rock light in 1875 and Langness Lighthouse in 1880.

Nicknamed the Manx Eddystone, Chicken Rock was a major achievement in rock-light building, and that would have been tribute enough to these sons of Robert. But David and Thomas also include in their list of lighthouses Muckle Flugga, which marks the northernmost outcrop of the British Isles, so wild that great waves can sweep up and over its 200-foot-high rock. And it was David and Thomas, too, who built the lighthouse on Dubh Artach, a solitary and vicious black jut of rock twelve miles off the southwest tip of the Isle of Mull.

Robert Louis Stevenson, son of Thomas, described Dubh Artach as 'one oval nodule of black trap, sparsely bedabbled with an inconspicuous fungus and alive in every crevice with a dingy insect between a slater and a bug. No other life was there but that of sea birds, and of the sea itself, that here ran like a mill race, and growled about the outer reef for ever and ever, and again, in the calmnest weather, roared and spouted on the rock itself.'

Earraid, a tiny island off the Ross of Mull, was chosen as the base

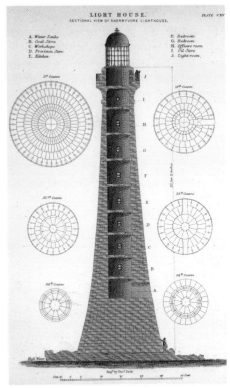

Plan of Skerryvore Lighthouse.

for operations for the Dubh Artach Lighthouse as there was good granite there for quarrying. Work began in April 1868. A barracks was built on the rock itself, as for the Bell Rock and Skerryvore — a round hutment of iron set on an apparently flimsy iron latticework base. Steam power had replaced some of the terrible physical labour linked with the earlier rock-light enterprises, but the engineers and the builders were as ever at the mercy of unpredictable winds and violent seas of such a force that on the rock stones dressed and ready for building and weighing over two tons were washed away in storms, like so many pebbles. Even Robert Stevenson at the Bell Rock had not known such force of sea.

Undaunted by the terrifying conditions, the builders, living for the best part of several building seasons in their curious spindly barracks, completed the lighthouse in 1872, and on 1 November of that year the now-resident keepers lit the light. The top of the iron barracks structure was removed, but the iron framework on which it had been set was only removed with considerable difficulty almost one hundred years later to make way for a helicopter pad.

Before his death in 1818, George Dempster of Dunnichen commented that before long 'the whole northern seas [would be] illuminated like Pall Mall from sunrise to sunset'. He would never know how very near the truth his jest had become within a hundred years of that first Commissioners' meeting. That earnest group of well-meaning men must often have thanked the Lord for the blessing and good fortune in finding the great and brave men who helped them set up their first lights. They, too, would never know how well that good fortune held for their successors.

But no matter how magnificent Thomas Smith's and the succession of Stevensons' contributions were in the design and the building of the lighthouses in that first hundred years, their efforts would have been to little effect if they had not devoted an equal energy to the development, research and building of the best of lights and to finding the best of men to care for them.

Building work on the Chicken Rock Lighthouse in progress.

Dubh Artach Lighthouse in progress.

LETTING THE LIGHT SO SHINE

Right from its very inception, the Northern Lighthouse Board appears to have had the knack of attracting men of a particular calibre to the work of manning the lights. Or perhaps it is the demands of the job itself that produces the calibre in the men. Whichever is the truth of the matter, the demands of lightkeeping would soon demonstrate to a man whether or not he can tolerate the almost unique conditions of work imposed by a lighthouse, and by rock lighthouses in particular. It was, and remains, a curious life of combined isolation and intimate proximity. As a modern keeper has expressed it, for weeks on end the world is 'an upright tube containing a madding crowd of three!'

For two hundred years the Board and their lights have been served by succeeding generations of courageous, self-reliant men not only dedicated to the work of keeping the lights but willing to work in some of the most isolated — if often very beautiful — places in the Kingdom, and often to risk life and limb getting to and from the job.

The earliest keepers were recruited by Thomas Smith and Robert Stevenson. Knowing better than most, and certainly rather more intimately than even the Commissioners, the conditions under which the lightkeepers and their families would have to exist, the early Engineers, and their successors in the 19th century, worked endlessly to try to make conditions of service and living as tolerable as possible.

It was Smith who recruited the first Northern Lighthouse keeper, as we have seen. James Park's conditions of employment set the pattern for what was to be standard practice for many years to come. The keeper and his family would live beside the light wherever possible. The lodging would be free and self-sufficiency in food would be encouraged, not only by the provision of grazing but, in some of the very remote areas, of small crofts. Every possible lighthouse would have garden ground provided, enclosed by protective walls. At the shore stations for the families of men serving out on the isolated rocks there would be gardens of considerable size.

When Thomas Smith appointed James Park, who was a former mariner, there was also begun another long tradition in the service, that of giving preference for employment to men with sea knowledge and skills. The first keeper at Eilean Glas was also a former sailor — a married man with a family who sailed to the lighthouse with him and set up home in what turned out to be an entirely inadequate house for the elements it was intended to withstand.

Thomas Smith, Robert and Alan Stevenson and their successors were deeply religious men, and as the lightkeeping staff grew under their surveillance it was natural that the men they selected for the hard life of lightkeeping had to measure up to the Engineers' high moral standards. In return for doing their duty well, the recruits were told, they would have not only great spiritual satisfaction but would find themselves life members of a caring 'family'. True to the prevailing spirit of the 19th century, spiritual reward was set on a somewhat higher plane than financial gain! Lighthouse-keeping took on some of the aura of a vocation and like any other vocation was beyond price, which was, no doubt, of little comfort to a keeper with many little mouths to feed. For the first few years the annual salary remained at £30, rising only very slowly to £45 in 1815. Almost sixty years later, in 1873, wages paid to lighthouse keepers was standardized through the United Kingdom, and Principal Keepers were then paid from £56 to

John Reid, first keeper of the Bell Rock Lighthouse.

£62. Men who served on the rock stations received always an extra allowance, and these were handsome enough to encourage some family men to stay at rock stations for many years. But the job also gave a man, and his family, a roof over their heads, their fuel and candles, land for a cow, a new uniform every three years, and a good standing in the community, not to mention a small pension and, from the early years of the 19th century, life assurance.

In 1836 Parliament passed an Act to make the building of further lights by the Commissioners subject to the approval of Trinity House in order to attain some 'uniformity of system in the management of lighthouses'. That year a deputation of the Elder Brethren of Trinity House visited the Scottish lights and were generally impressed not only by the quality of the lights and the lamps but also by the keepers. Perhaps they realized somewhat ruefully that their own system may have lacked a certain uniformity, but the Scottish system certainly did not. In England there had been, for instance, no uniformity of building policy and no standard criteria set for staff recruitment.

Sir Henry Pelly, one of the party who toured the Scottish lights, wrote, 'The Northern Lightkeepers were certainly an intelligent and respectable class of men, for their station in life. . . . Their respective plots of ground, forming part of their emolument, not only fixes them to the soil, but gives them a status in the country as Small Farmers and their Life Assurance is now looked forward to as an Inheritance connected with the Lighthouse service; nor is the uniform clothing furnished to them to be overlooked in adding to their respectability in localities where in their circumstances a decent dress is not to be had for money.'

SHORE STATIONS

As the number of lights steadily grew, so did the need to provide adequate accommodation for the families of the men, particularly those on rock stations who were away for sometimes months at a time. It was early recognized that a man in isolation could be expected to give of his best only if he had as few domestic worries as possible.

Some of the shore stations were well placed in coastal towns such as Campbeltown and Stromness, Arbroath and Leith. Others were almost as isolated as the rock stations themselves. Earraid Shore Station was one such. Set on a tiny dot of an island off the Ross of Mull, this was the site where stones were quarried and cut for the building of Dubh Artach. Robert Louis Stevenson described the activity on Earraid at that time: 'There was now a pier of stone, there were rows of sheds, railways, travelling cranes, a street of cottages, an iron house for the resident engineers, wooden bothies for the men, a stage where the courses of the tower were put together experimentally, and behind the settlement a great gash in the hillside where the granite was quarried.'

When Dubh Artach was finished, the site at Earraid was turned into a shore station, the families living in the 'street of cottages' — solid granite houses suited to the rough climate. The Dubh Artach families moved in immediately and were joined by the Skerryvore keepers' families twenty years later when Hynish Shore Station was closed. At that time a little schoolroom was tacked on at the end of the street.

Thomas Stevenson (1818-87) by Sir John Reid.

Left, the Dubh Artach workyard on the island of Earraid. Right, Robert Louis Stevenson (1850-94) by Count Girolamo Neri.

A sense of isolation pervaded the little isle of Earraid, even when eight families lived there. And that sense is nowhere better conjured up than by Robert Louis Stevenson in *Kidnapped.* The hero, David Balfour, after the shipwreck of the *Covenant,* is washed up on Earraid: 'There was no one part of it better than another; it was all desolate and rocky; nothing lived on it but game birds which I lacked the means to kill, and the gulls which haunted the outlying rocks in a prodigious manner. But the creek, or strait, that cut off the isle from the mainland of Ross, opened out on the North into a bay, and the bay again opened into the Sound of Iona. . . .

'Now, from a little up the hillside over the bay, I could catch a sight of the great ancient church and the roofs of the people's houses in Iona. And on the other hand, over the low country of the Ross, I saw smoke go up, morning and evening, as if from homesteads.'

It could never have been easy to raise a family with all the intrinsic health and educational problems in places that are not only remote but exceedingly difficult to reach even today.

As we have already seen, at the very beginning of the service only one keeper was appointed to each lighthouse, and it must have been essential for him to have had a wife or a grown-up family to help him in those early years. The first official Assistant Lightkeepers were appointed in 1815, and eventually most of the lighthouses had a staff of three — a Principal Keeper and two Assistants — or four where there was a foghorn to be operated. At stations inaccessible by road, Attending Boatmen, usually local fishermen, were also recruited to the service, being paid retainers to serve the keepers and their men. These boatmen were often a very real lifeline to the families at the very isolated lights. Gradually, as the need arose, there evolved the roles of relief keepers, occasional keepers, and part-time attendant keepers.

Since the supreme duty was to show the light in the hours of darkness, an all-night watch on the light had to be mounted. A shift system at night was devised, akin to watches on board ship, and it was required that one man be on duty in the daytime to tend to the light, the fuel, the trimming of the lamp, the polishing, while the other cleaned the lightroom, the windows, and so on.

In addition, from the very earliest times a record was kept daily of the weather conditions, fuel consumption and anything else of significance, all of which had to be reported to the Engineers and by them to the Board, or else sent directly to the Board's headquarters in Edinburgh. Some of these records formed the basis of the study of British weather by the embryo meteorologists of the mid-19th century, usually men of the cloth and lesser college professors who were all persistent correspondents with the Trustees, demanding access to the weather records put together by the keepers.

Originally the keepers were instructed in their work with the actual lights by the Engineers, but in 1810 the Board appointed its very first Superintendent of Lightkeepers' Duties — John Forrest. He was succeeded in 1824 by Lachlan Kennedy, who had been clerk to the engineers at the building of the Bell Rock light. Thus at this early stage, too, was established another lighthouse tradition of promoting men of experience from the 'ranks'.

It was reported that the year after the opening of the Bell Rock light, the keepers had had to receive many visitors, and it became — and remains — a part of the keepers' duties to admit visitors to the lighthouse in the afternoon and up until an hour before lighting time, provided this does not disrupt essential work. There were times when this could develop into a considerable nuisance and a threat to the smooth operation of a station. In 1848, for instance, the Commissioners were very perturbed by newspaper advertisements offering picnic excursions to Inchkeith. A General Order was sent round all the lights instructing that should they be visited by large crowds then the lightroom was not to be open to inspection.

In return for doing their duty, keepers certainly had a certain security working for the Board, which operated, for example, a kind of health-care service by which a doctor in a locality was paid a retainer by the Board to attend to the keepers and their families. If a doctor had to be called, a small sum had to be paid by the keeper for his attendance, but the Board ensured that at least the doctor would feel obliged to call. This arrangement did not, however, cover visits attendant upon births to keepers' wives. The total cost of these had to be met by the keepers.

There was, of course, one enormous flaw in this plan. The sheer distance from habitation and the inaccessibility, except by boat, of some of the stations could make the calling out of a doctor, given there was one in the area, something of a daunting venture for all concerned. Lighthouse-keepers' wives, even today, who have memories of a remote station such as Earraid will talk at length about the terrors of illness in such places and of the wonderful bonds created amongst families who often had only each other to count on for help in times of desperate trouble or serious accident.

THE 1886 REPORT

A century ago, the incidence of tuberculosis amongst the keepers and their families was a matter of considerable concern to the Commissioners. In 1883, they approached a Professor Madigan to make a report on lightkeepers' health. Among matters the professor was asked to investigate was whether or not the men already in the service were of a sufficiently robust frame for the duties they had to

Elevation of the Signal Tower for the Bell Rock Lighthouse with the keepers' houses below, from Robert Stevenson's Account.

SHEWING THE HOURS FOR LIGHTING AND EXTINGUISHING,

Note.—The Tabular Numbers are the Times of Sunset and Sunri...

FEBRUARY Time of Extinguishing	Time of Lighting	Day of the Month	MARCH Time of Extinguishing	Time of Lighting	Day of the Month	APRIL Time of Extinguishing
Hrs. Mins.	Hrs. Mins.		Hrs. Mins.	Hrs. Mins.		Hrs. Mins.
8 · 8	4 · 40	1	7 · 4	5 · 41	1	5 · 41
8 · 6	4 · 43	2	7 · 1	5 · 43	2	5 · 38
8 · 3	4 · 45	3	6 · 58	5 · 45	3	5 · 36
8 · 1	4 · 48	4	6 · 56	5 · 48	4	5 · 33
7 · 59	4 · 50	5	6 · 53	5 · 50	5	5 · 30
7 · 57	4 · 52	6	6 · 50	5 · 52	6	5 · 28
7 · 55	4 · 55	7	6 · 48	5 · 54	7	5 · 25
7 · 52	4 · 57	8	6 · 45	5 · 57	8	5 · 22
7 · 50	5 · 0	9	6 · 42	5 · 59	9	5 · 19
7 · 48	5 · 2	10	6 · 39	6 · 1	10	5 · 16
7 · 46	5 · 4	11	6 · 37	6 · 4	11	5 · 14
7 · 44	5 · 6	12	6 · 34	6 · 6	12	5 · 12
7 · 41	5 · 8	13	6 · 31	6 · 8	13	5 · 9
7 · 39	5 · 10	14	6 · 29	6 · 10	14	5 · 7
7 · 34	5 · 12	15	6 · 26	6 · 12	15	5 · 4
7 · 35	5 · 14	16	6 · 23	6 · 14	16	5 · 2
7 · 33	5 · 16	17	6 · 20	6 · 16	17	5 · 0
7 · 31	5 · 18	18	6 · 18	6 · 19	18	4 · 57
7 · 28	5 · 20	19	6 · 15	6 · 21	19	4 · 55
7 · 26	5 · 22	20	6 · 12	6 · 23	20	4 · 52
7 · 24	5 · 24	21	6 · 10	6 · 25	21	4 · 50
7 · 21	5 · 26	22	6 · 7	6 · 27	22	4 · 48
7 · 18	5 · 28	23	6 · 4	6 · 29	23	4 · 45
7 · 16	5 · 30	24	6 · 2	6 · 31	24	4 · 43
7 · 14	5 · 32	25	5 · 59	6 · 33	25	4 · 40
7 · 11	5 · 35	26	5 · 57	6 · 35	26	4 · 38

The Table of times for 1856 at which the light at the Bell Rock Lighthouse was to be lit and extinguished every day, computed for the appropriate latitude.

perform and was there 'any tendency on the part of the lightkeepers to fancy themselves unhealthy and to take drugs which are unnecessary'. Above all, the Commissioners wanted to know if any improvement could be made in the methods of selecting candidates to the service.

The professor's report, made in 1886, reinforced the Board's concern about deaths from tuberculosis and blamed its high incidence on the contrast between the work keepers had to do in colder parts of the lighthouse with the hours spent in the stuffy hot lamprooms. He recommended that to make sure of recruiting robust men these should be taken on according to the physical standards required by the British artillery regiments. Their work, which included lifting heavy weights, corresponded well with the kind of work done by lightkeepers. A keeper ought, he considered, to be no shorter than five feet six inches, with a chest girth of 34 inches minimum, and weigh at least ten stones, in order to qualify for selection.

As to the matter of unnecessary drug-taking, the professor had checked the contents of the medicine chests provided for the keepers, and it was his opinion that the keepers were over-dosing themselves. There was distinct evidence of excess use of blue-pill morphia and quinine, but most of all the professor was struck by the large amount of purgative medicine being consumed — which was hardly surprising given the constipating effects of the morphia that was apparently being used to treat everything from sore throats to queasy stomachs!

Concern for the bodily health of the men was well complemented by the Board's care of their spiritual welfare. The devout Stevensons made certain the Commissioners were not allowed to overlook their duty — as the Stevensons saw it — to see to it that the men and their families could attend church services regularly when possible. But this was clearly impossible in such stations as Ruvaal on Islay where there was no access road of any kind, or on Lismore where the lighthouse was twelve miles from the parish church, or at the Mull of Kintyre where the round trip to a church would have taken so long there was a danger the lightkeeper might not get back to his light in time for duty. It became a rule, generally observed, that where a church was not near at hand then the Principal Lightkeepers conducted Sunday services. Even then, there was grave concern over the want of spiritual guidance and instruction for the young, not to mention baptism.

The practical solution to this problem was for the Commissioners, who had long had their own chaplain whose duties included the devising of special prayers for use at lighthouses, to appoint a missionary to travel round the lights. The Reverend George Easton, therefore, was appointed in 1852 and remained lighthouse missionary for 41 years, visiting each lighthouse, if possible, at least once a year and remaining up to four weeks at a time.

His report of his tour in 1866 shows that he spent no fewer than 181 days at lighthouses and shore stations, visiting keepers and their families, and regretting that bad weather had prevented him from visiting Barrahead. In his report the Reverend George dwells lightly on his own transport problems, goes into considerable detail over the distances from church the flock in his care find themselves and how the keepers cope with the instruction of their children. 'The children gathered together twice a day during my visit and the children's behaviour and attention to their lessons were all that I could have wished. Parents without exception [are] anxiously alive to the importance of the children's education.'

At Monach he reported that of the Principal's four children, 'the eldest fills a respectable situation in Leith. Three children at home are evidently educated and far advanced for their ages. The Assistant is likewise married with four young children. This man educates his own children.' Most of the Principals' First Assistants appear to have been married men — or if not, had a sister keeping house. At Fladda, the Assistant Keeper was unmarried, his sister keeping house not only for him but for a younger brother and sister living with them. Mr Easton comments, 'I cannot speak too highly of the careful attention this lightkeeper has for the last three years paid to the last two. They have received excellent education from him.'

On his tour Mr Easton also comes up with at least one practical solution to educational problems. At MacArthur's Head, the Principal's daughter was given the task of supervising the education of the Assistant's five children. Between the visit in March and the writing of the report at the year's end, the missionary had received specimens of the youngsters' handwriting and was delighted to say what he had seen had been excellent.

The Reverend Easton concludes his report by thanking the Commissioners for 'the Book of Prayers lately added to the growing libraries in Lighthouse establishments', and adding, 'I cannot close this report without acknowledging the great personal kindness and attention which I have received during another year at the hands of all the members of the Light House families I have been privileged to visit'.

The missionary's reference to the growing libraries at the light stations points to another matter that concerned the Trustees for decades last century. A Trinity House delegation in the 1840s had alluded to the want of books in the lighthouses, and the Commissioners were well aware not only of the problems facing keepers in educating their children in remote stations, but the value of good reading material — books and magazines — to keep the men of the service informed and occupied.

Advice was sought in 1847 from Mr William Graham, an Edinburgh English teacher, who advised *Maculloch's Series of Lessons* for the 5 to 9-year-olds. And for the older children *Maculloch's Course of Reading, Introduction to the Sciences*, Lennie's *English Grammar, History of the British Empire*, Stuart's *Geography*, and *The School Atlas*. He further recommended the *Geographical Primer* and *Primer Atlas*, with this comment: 'Geography would seem to me a very entertaining study in those lonely situations and to which the pupil would turn with interest in a place where he sees vessels from distant countries whose passing visits may be said to constitute the only variety of life.' Mr Graham further recommended Sir Walter Scott's *History of Scotland*, which he averred 'would beguile the tedium of a winter night and beget a love of reading'. The Commissioners agreed to the provision of a set of educational books for each family, and in December 1847 one hundred boxes of teaching books and copy books were purchased, each set costing 10 shillings and 8 pence (53 pence).

Nineteen years later, the question of supplying other books and periodicals still had not been solved, and a committee was formed in November 1866 to investigate. Not for the first time, a plan was evolved to institute a peripatetic library. The old and tried idea of sending out a box of volumes to each lighthouse annually, recalling it and renewing it each year, was aired and rejected. The plan had not worked before, and now the cost would be prohibitive. The solution was found in a proposal to set up a library at each station by sending annually two new books. These volumes would in time make up a resident library in each lighthouse, even although each volume must have been thoroughly well thumbed by the end of a twelvemonth.

In addition, the coast was divided into nine separate areas, and to each lighthouse in an area it was arranged to send at regular intervals 'two magazines for the adults and three small publications for the wives and children', demonstrating in one revealing phrase not only the Commissioners' care for the families but their consideration of the place of women in their Victorian scheme of things. Where there were more than two keepers at a station, an extra bundle was to be sent.

As examples of the magazines that were to be ordered, proposed for Area 1 were *The Family Treasury* and *Leisure Hour* for the keepers and *British Workman*, *Mother's Treasury* and *Lamp of Love* for the wives and children. And that would have been a slightly jollier monthly prospect than the order for Area 4 which was to be *Spurgeon's Sermons* in monthly parts for the keepers and *The Band of Hope Review*, *Old Jonathan* and *The Children's Friend* for the wives and children. The twenty Attending Boatmen in the service who would have the job of delivering the packages to their stations were to be supplied with one magazine and three small periodicals each.

Even the Commissioners at their General Meeting protested that although the idea was an excellent one, some of the reading material was pretty heavy going, and they suggested a slight leavening of the content. Over and above the magazines to be provided to the lighthouses, it was further proposed to send each a copy of the quarterly magazine *The Lifeboat*, and the scheme was approved.

CHANGING CONDITIONS

By 1885, it is evident from the Board's records that in the near hundred years since the first lightkeepers and their families had taken up residence at lighthouses the Commissioners had had to do a deal of rethinking on what could reasonably be expected in the way of duty and service by a man with family cares.

At several remote stations keepers complained that the land which had been given them, with the intention of letting it provide the family with fresh food and with grazing for a cow or the keeping of cattle for the provision of fresh meat, had become exhausted with overuse. Often enough there had been complaints of crop destruction by storms or simply by adverse conditions at seed time or at harvest. But towards their first centenary the Trustees were becoming more and more aware of the problem of land exhaustion, and the matter was urgent when one remembers that the land provided was considered part of a keeper's income. The first response of the Board was to ask the keepers who complained to secure accurate reports on the condition of their soils from practical agriculturalists, at the keepers' own expense. In due course all reports were forthcoming, and they almost all demonstrated the keepers' claims were well founded.

It is difficult to tell at this distance in time how much the Victorian fashion for large families had to do with this pressure on the soil, but the problem did give rise to a considerable rethinking of the housing and allotment provisions at the remote stations. Increasingly, towards the end of their first century the Commissioners rehoused men and their families at shore stations in or near coastal towns and villages, where provisions could be bought to supplement the diet provided by the land, but probably an even greater impetus towards this change were the Education Acts of 1872 and 1873, providing compulsory public education for all.

A system of public parish education had been a fact of Scottish life for over three hundred years, which is why the Commissioners had been prepared to spend so much money in the 1840s on primers and copybooks for lighthouse children, but the 1870s Acts meant education was no longer a matter of choice but of law, and the Board was confronted by a considerable problem. As far as possible, men with families were stationed near schooling, and where this was not possible, or where a child had attained a higher grade of education, boarding allowances were eventually paid by the Board. The Board in due course found itself paying out fairly handsomely for the boarding out of children of high attainment. Lighthouse children were — and are — achievers!

As standards of living improved in the second half of the 19th century, although not too much could be done to improve conditions of living in the rock lighthouses, there was concern over the inadequacy of some of the housing provided for the keepers and their families. At Girdle Ness, for instance, it was reported in 1886 that because the original two houses for Assistant Keepers had had to be converted into three houses, the accommodation was 'quite insufficient for any keeper who is married and has children and in arranging for the transfer of keepers, care has to be taken to select young men without families for a station which is among the best and most suitable for educational purposes of any in the service'.

The planned development of the North Berwick Shore Station in the same year, 1886, indicates also the Commissioners' policy in the establishment of shore stations. In this instance it might have been cheaper to have acquired available housing in different parts of the town to house the Firth of Forth keepers' families, but it was decided that 'it would not be advantageous to the discipline of the Station to have the 3 keepers in houses in different parts of the town'. Not a little of this notion of retaining discipline was reflected in the pecking order that seems to have appeared at these stations amongst the womenfolk, whereby number one woman was the Principal Lightkeeper's wife and the rest followed in descending order of rank.

A letter in the Board's archives, dated 17 June 1885, demonstrates very clearly indeed how ideas were changing and had changed since the early days when living conditions were little considered and Robert Stevenson in particular had had to spend a deal of time and energy persuading the Board to improve keepers' conditions of employment, provide pensions and rewards for long service and for effort above and beyond the call of duty, and give them reasonably sound homes to live in. The letter is addressed to J.M. Duncan, Secretary of the Northern Lighthouse Board, from Robert Muirhead, the Board's Superintendent:

'Dear Sir, As I understand that the Board of Trade will be inclined to consider favourably the proposed transfer of the Chickens Rock Shore Station from the Calf of Man to Port St Mary if satisfied that such a change be for the benefit of the service, I beg to call your attention particularly to the following points — 1st — The disadvantages of having 4 lightkeepers' families on an Island distant about 5 miles, by sea, from the nearest town, with all its concurrent boating risks and inconveniences — 2nd — The danger of having so many women and children practically out of reach of the Doctor — 3rd — The disadvantages which the Keepers labour under through having no schooling for their children — 4th — The size and condition of the present dwelling houses and 5th — The condition of the landing place at the Calf of Man.

'1st. The Calf of Man lies about 5 miles West of Port St Mary, the nearest town, where Kelly the Attending Boatman resides, and the boat is kept. Thus the lightkeepers' families are practically dependent on the regularity of the boat trips for their provisions and proper maintenance. . . . Kelly the boatman is paid an annual salary of £60 (including £8 for house rent) and the crew get 11/- [shillings] for each provision trip; the boat pay bill under this heading amounted to £14 18/- in the year 1884. . . . To make these trips in one day is sometimes no easy matter, especially in winter or even in summer with contrary winds. Hence the boat often does not get away from the Calf on its final return to Port St Mary till darkness has set in, when it is impossible to see a coming squall ere it has reached and imperilled the boat. In consequence of this and for the safety of himself and crew, Kelly has intimated that he is to apply to have two days allowed for performing these trips. This moderate request, if granted, will add at least 4/- fortnightly or £5 4/- annually to the Boat attendance charges.

'All the 4 Lightkeepers' houses on the Calf are about 1½ miles from the landing place, and on the arrival of the boat, outward to the Rock, the Keepers' clothes, provisions etc. have to be carted down to the boat, while on return homeward, the empty boxes etc. brought from the rock have to be carted up to the houses. A sum of £15 is paid annually for performing this work, and also carting the Keepers' annual supply of coal.

'2nd. There are at present 27 persons living on the Calf of Man (including the 3 Keepers on duty on the rock) and with such a number, mostly women and children, there always is a certain amount of sickness. . . . It may be said that only Keepers who have no families should be selected for stations like these. But there are very few unmarried men in the service and still fewer suitable for Rock Stations, as I prefer to have a year or two's experience of a man's capabilities and health qualifications before sending him to a rock and ere this time of probation be passed he will certainly be married.

'4th. The houses at the Calf of Man are without exception the smallest in the service. . . . In the Principal's house there are at present 10 people resident, and taking the Cubic Air space at 3363 feet it gives only 336 feet per head which is much too little. The Board of Supervision recommends at least 400 feet per head in lodging houses, 600 feet per head is allowed in barracks and 560 feet is the minimum allowed to each prisoner in Edinburgh Jail.

'5th. As I have quite lately reported on the dangerous condition of the landing place at the Calf of Man it is needless to say more on this point here. But I think it would be a pity to spend at least £100 putting it into proper order at present. For the sum of £15 the most dangerous of the rocks could be removed and the risk for the present considerably lessened. However, should it be decided to retain the Chickens Rock Shore Station at the Calf a large expenditure of money will be necessary to secure the safety of the men's lives.'

LIGHTS, BUOYS & BEACONS

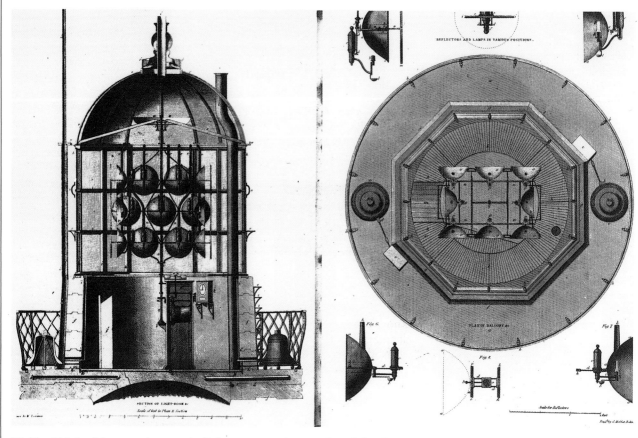

Unlike Trinity House, whose early lights were a mixture of coal-fired beacons, candles and rudimentary oil lamps, the Northern Lighthouse Board's very first lights were oil lamps, and as soon as they took over the Isle of May light in 1815 the coal beacon there was dismantled and an oil light installed.

Thomas Smith's earliest successful lights were adaptations of Aimé Argand's oil lamps, with wicks burning whale oil and the light improved by a reflector made of faceted mirror glass, which looked a little like a much magnified image of a fly's eye. The light produced was static and diffuse and did not exhibit any individual character, that is, any characteristic to distinguish it from other lights. Smith's first attempt to differentiate lights came when he built a smaller lantern below the Pladda light in the Clyde, so that the resulting double light would not be mistaken for the light on the Mull of Kintyre or the Copeland Light in Northern Ireland.

Robert Stevenson was an indefatigable traveller in search of better lights. It was his firm opinion that copper plated with silver and used as reflectors gave a much better light than mirrors. When he visited the St Agnes Light off the Scillies in 1801, he noticed with interest that the revolving light there was producing three flashes, of which two were brighter than the third. When he examined the light, he discovered that two of the reflectors were parabolic in shape while the third was of conical design. Not only did this indicate to Stevenson the superiority of the parabolic reflector, it also seemed a useful means of producing a form of light identification.

Section and plan for the light and the lightroom beneath at the Bell Rock Lighthouse, from Robert Stevenson's An Account of the Bell Rock Lighthouse.

Scotland's first revolving light was installed at Start Point, on Sanday in the Orkneys, in 1806.

There was further experimenting for identification purposes using coloured glass, and the Bell Rock Lighthouse was the first in Scotland to have distinguishing alternating red and white beams, produced by twenty-four silvered metal reflectors mounted on a rectangular frame — seven down each long side and five on each short side, those on the shorter sides having additional red glass shades.

In 1820 Robert Stevenson took his two eldest sons, Alan and Bob, on the inspection tour on the Lighthouse yacht *Pharos*. The tour ended with a visit to the coast of France as far south as the entrance to the Gironde, where stands the famous Tour de Cordouan. This great lighthouse, over 197 feet high, was begun in 1584 and completed in 1610. Its age and dimensions were astonishing enough to Robert, but what was particularly impressive was the intensity of the light — from an oil lamp completely surrounded by an arrangement of prisms.

Robert Stevenson wasted no time in getting in touch with the inventor, Augustin Fresnel, in Paris, and there began a long and fruitful friendship and an open sharing of information that was to become the hallmark of lighthouse engineering. Stevenson and his descendants, Fresnel's and his, shared a common philosophy that if there was a chance of their improvements saving lives then these improvements had to become common knowledge.

Improvements and changes came thick and fast in the 19th century. The first flashing light was installed in Scotland at Buchan Ness in 1827, and at about the same time occulting lights were introduced, in which the light is made to flash intermittently by being covered for a short time. All of this was to help in the problem of distinguishing lights one from another, a problem that increased with the number of lighthouses completed.

Robert Stevenson was a pretty determined character, to the point, claim his detractors, of being too stubbornly sure of his own ideas to accept readily new suggestions. In the matter of trying to get the best possible light, this was patently not so. The 1830s was a period of concentrated experiment with glass prisms both to refract and reflect light — all with Robert's encouragement.

In due course the catoptric or reflecting system, favoured in Scotland until then, gave way to the refracting dioptric lens system which was installed first at the Inchkeith Light in the River Forth in 1835, after exhaustive experiments had been carried out by Robert's son and new partner, Alan. The experiments proved that fully one-third more light was transmitted by means of the glass prisms than by polished metal surfaces.

Neither Robert's system of double lights — one placed above the other — nor the use of coloured lights was sufficient answer to the problem of identification, and Robert was very quick to accept the possibilities of timing light beams to produce varying identifying intermittence by means of Fresnel's lens framework which revolved around a lamp. It was a relatively simple matter to have sections blanked off to provide the correct interval between the beams.

Eventually there evolved the use of individual panels of prisms, producing pencil beams revolving at speeds and in patterns made known to mariners. From 1840 onwards, the size and complexity of these lenses were increased in an effort to make the most of the comparatively limited light source available from oil lamps.

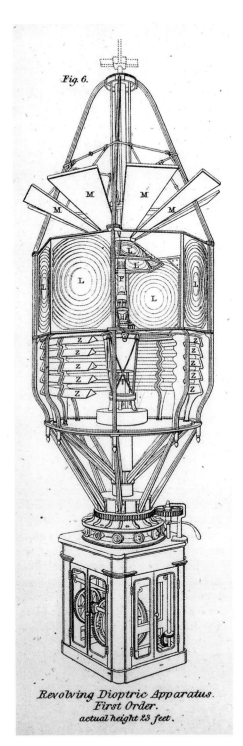

Fig. 6.

Revolving Dioptric Apparatus.
First Order.
actual height 23 feet.

The clockwork mechanism devised for revolving these lights and prisms is awesomely simple. Driven by a weight which gradually descends to the foot of the tower from the lamp room, the lenses revolve at the required speed — originally on metal rollers. These weights required to be wound up to the top again hourly or so. Today's rotating lights float on a bath of mercury, and the clockwork is driven by a tiny motor. All is so accurately set that the push of a finger can set the lenses revolving despite, in some cases, weighing several tons.

The first fuels used by the Northern Lighthouse Board were the fairly crude whale oil or finer sperm-whale oil. Later, after much persuasion by a member of parliament called Joseph Hume, of whom more anon, the Board turned for a time to colza oil, which is produced from oil-seed rape. The problem with both of these early oils was the unreliability of supply as well as quality. Despite Dundee and Leith's importance in the whaling industry, the supply and cost of whale oil was always a great imponderable to the Commissioners, who carefully put their requirements out to tender. And since colza oil had, at that time, to be imported, the supply and price of it, too, could never be completely assured.

The eventual solution to the fuel problem turned up almost literally on the Commissioners' Edinburgh doorstep. Around 1847 Mr James Young, experimenting with shale of which there were huge deposits in West Lothian and Midlothian, extracted the petroleum fuel paraffin, from the crude mineral oil produced by the shale. As the price of paraffin dropped, the lighthouse oil lamps were gradually replaced by paraffin burners, which produced a bright light from a mantle fuelled by paraffin vapourized under pressure.

Another development mid-century was the general progress in the coal gas industry, and in a very few lighthouses near a town supply gas lighting was installed. Later, electric light was the object of much experimentation, and in 1885 the Northern Lighthouse Board began installing its first electric light on the Isle of May. The May electric light was a carbon-arc lamp that produced an extraordinarily bright light and required several hundred feet of carbon a year, not to mention the work of six, instead of the normal three, keepers. The May electric light had the refinement — devised by Thomas Stevenson, father of Robert Louis — of being able to dip downwards in poor visibility to intensify the light shed on the waters surrounding the dangerous shore. The Isle of May electric light was first lit on 1 December 1886, marking one hundred years of steady development that had multiplied the brightness of the Northern Lights almost a thousandfold — a brilliance Thomas Smith might have wished for only in his wildest dreams.

BUOYS AND BEACONS

From earliest times coastal towns and villages had felt it incumbent upon themselves to provide landmarks and shore beacons for the benefit of their homecoming sailors. Even in modern times, with sophisticated navigational aids, sailors still happily line up safe harbour approaches by means of church towers and clefts in headlands, a reliable enough daytime, fair-weather tactic that only occasionally fails, as when, in recent times, for instance, a Scottish west coast church was demolished, spire and all, and for weeks there was bafflement on the high seas!

Buoys marking sunken ships, buoys locating sandbanks or rock shallows, buoys marking deep-water estuary channels, are all essential to the safety of mariners, but responsibility for these was not part of the original brief of the Northern Lighthouse Board. In the early years, the Commissioners were concerned there should be no confusion between their lighthouses and other beacons and warnings on the coast. The steadily increasing sea trade in the early years of the 19th century — trade that was a vital link in the distribution chain of products pouring from the new industrial heartland of Scotland — and the mounting totals of ships and sailors lost in storms around the coasts, made the proper management of sea marks a matter of great concern.

Anything, including landmarks, that would make the sea approaches safer was of interest to the Commissioners, to the extent, on occasion, of finding money from their fund to help projects with seemingly little connection with their work. In 1805 they gave £300 towards rebuilding the steeple of Inveresk Church on the south shore of the Firth of Forth, and in 1809 and 1814 they voted 100 guineas (£105) to help the completion of Nelson's Monument on Calton Hill in Edinburgh. The monument, curiously like an almost folded telescope, is still a discernible landmark on the river approach to Leith.

The entrance to the River Forth was of continuing concern to the Board. Whereas the setting up of buoys in the Clyde was the responsibility of the Clyde Lighthouse Authority and Dundee looked after the Tay, there was no one generally responsible for the Forth. The North Carr rocks that Admiral Cochrane had referred to in his letter about the Bell Rock in 1793 were marked by the first Northern Lighthouse Board buoy in 1809. This buoy was a comparatively crude affair, moored by ropes. It was not until 1840 that wrought-iron chains were used for mooring, first of all at the Culloden Rock in the Moray Firth.

By 1828 the Commissioners had taken over the management and maintenance of several buoys in the Forth, but it was not until the Act of 1838, following a Parliamentary Select Committee investigation into the whole comprehensive question of British lights, buoys, beacons, and so on, that the Commissioners were given power to establish beacons and buoys where they thought necessary.

In the ensuing years, the Board placed unlit and lit beacons and buoys, marking rocks and sandbanks, in almost every firth and sound in the kingdom. For the first fifty years, despite much experimentation with luminous paint and later with electrically lit buoys, whose chief snag was the placing of power cables, no truly practical means of lighting buoys was discovered until the 1880s when one Julius Pintsch devised a means of doing so with compressed oil gas. Lamps thus lit required to be refuelled at six-monthly intervals only.

In a report made to the 12th International Congress of Navigation in Philadelphia in 1912, David A. Stevenson, the fifth successive member of the family to be Engineer to the Commissioners, reported: 'The recharging is affected [sic] by a vessel going alongside the buoy carrying a reservoir of compressed oil gas and through a hose, the gas is allowed to flow into the buoy, or forced into it by a compressor. This operation can be performed with safety, even in moderately rough weather.'

FOGHORNS AND THE FLEET

The long want of the right technology not only affected the lighting of buoys but also hampered the devising of adequate fog warning signals. The bell on the Bell Rock served that purpose long before and after the lighthouse was built. In other parts of the country, fog warnings were provided by cannon and shotgun fire.

One of the Board's General Managers, Alexander Cuningham, made a particular study of fog signalling in various conditions. He proposed a variety of solutions in the 1860s — warning gongs at harbour mouths, gunfire on the main stretches of coast, horns in bays and inlets. His ideas were based on the two principal requirements of fog signalling — that the signal be heard over the largest possible distance and that each signal be distinguishable from the others. In 1876 the Board installed its first siren fog signal at St Abb's Head — a loud siren driven by hot air. Soon the coast was to resound to the characteristic booming horns of the lighthouse fog warnings.

The crew of the North Carr *lightvessel.*

The effectiveness of lightships had been demonstrated at the building of the Bell Rock, when the Prussian fishing vessel *Tonge Gerrit* had been converted into living quarters for the men and, with lights hoisted atop, had served as a warning to ships in the area. It was not, however, until 1877 that the Board acquired again this weapon in their ever-growing safety armoury. The first lightship was the *Abertay*, anchored at the entrance to the Firth of Tay marking dangerous sandbanks. In 1887 a second lightvessel complete with fog signal was anchored on the north side of the entrance to the Forth, marking the notorious North Carr rocks at Fifeness.

When the service began, Thomas Smith, and then Robert Stevenson, travelled the coasts surveying, visiting the new lights, in a variety of vessels hired when necessary, and sometimes at their own expense. But once several lighthouses were in operation, the Board were faced with the necessity of setting up a regular provisioning service. They simply could no longer depend on local hirers to provide the kind of craft necessary for the work, nor, in the very remote areas, could they even depend on there being local hirers, far less boats large enough to use as tenders. The solution was obvious — to build, or convert, ships for the purpose.

The Northern Lighthouse Board's very first tender, to be called *Pharos*, was not in fact the Bell Rock lightship converted from a trawler, but a sloop built in Elie in Fife and bought by Thomas Smith and presented to the service in 1799. Smith, well aware by then of the hard work and dangers in servicing even the handful of lights at that time, had the boat fitted out with particular care for the job it had to do and for the crew who manned her. It was on this first *Pharos* that Robert Stevenson made his fact-finding tour of English lighthouses in 1801, and the same ship took Stevenson and Smith north in the following year to begin the light at Start Point in the Orkneys.

The demands of the service soon outstripped the provisioning abilities of *Pharos*, and in December 1805 she was sold, her place taken for a time by a hired schooner, *Stromness*. In 1807 the lightship/tender *Pharos* was joined on the Bell Rock work by the sloop *Smeaton*, specially ordered by the Commissioners and named after the builder of the Eddystone Light, and soon afterwards by the new schooner, *Sir Joseph Banks*, and by two more sloops, *Patriot* and *Alexander*. The 38-ton *Pharos* the second was built at Leith in 1816 and based there as tender to the Bell Rock Lighthouse, but in 1841 was joined on that run by the *Prince of Wales*. To begin with, the *Pharos* doubled as the Engineer's ship for his tour of inspection, but in 1819 the *Regent* was built for general lighthouse work, carrying stores and accommodating Commissioners on their visits to lighthouses.

The very first lighthouse steamship was the wooden paddle steamer *Skerryvore*, built at Leith in 1839 and based at Hynish on Tiree during the building of the Skerryvore Lighthouse. She was sold in 1843. *Regent* was replaced in 1846 by the third *Pharos*. A London-built iron paddle steamer, she was in service for only five years when the Commissioners acquired *Pharos* number four, a ship almost twice as big. The fifth *Pharos* followed in 1874, another iron paddle steamer and the fleet's flagship, based at Granton which had replaced Leith by this time as the principal stores depot for the Lighthouse Board.

Meantime, other lesser ships and storage hulks had come and gone — the sloops *Thames* and *Argyle*, *Skerryvore II*; the iron paddle steamers *Dhuheartach*, used for the building of the Dubh Artach light, and *Terrible*, who ended her days driven ashore on Earraid.

Just as, from its very inception, lighthouse service became a tradition in some families, so did service on the Board's ships. Often, too, men who had worked as keepers became crewmen on tenders — and who better to appreciate the appalling difficulties of landing men and stores in adverse sea and weather conditions from launches whose only power sources were strong arms and oars.

THE COMMISSIONERS

In 1886 Britain annexed Upper Burma, the Irish Home Rule Bill was defeated in the Commons, Daimler produced his first motor car, the Canadian Pacific Railway was completed, gold was discovered in the Transvaal, every town and village in the kingdom was abustle with plans and preparations for Queen Victoria's Golden Jubilee in the following year, and on 1 August the Northern Lighthouse Board was one hundred years old.

A centenary would seem an apposite time to reflect on past achievements, but in the Minutes of General and Committee Meetings and in General Order and Correspondence books of that year it seems there was no time for sentimental reflection. Everyone was beavering away over new lights and technical developments, discussing the problems of keepers and their families, being bothered about excursionists making nuisances of themselves on Ailsa Craig, abandoning the idea of a bridge to link Earraid to the Ross of Mull because the Duke of Argyll was agin the notion, looking out for property at Girvan for the housing of the families of the new keepers for the Ailsa Craig gas light and also seeking property to rehouse the Calf of Man families, as Superintendent Muirhead had advised.

They had to deal, too, with some dissension in the ranks. There was a petition from a great number of keepers protesting against a recent ban on reading and writing in the lightroom. The ban had been occasioned by an incident the previous November when a keeper had become so absorbed in his book — surely not *Spurgeon's Sermons* — that he had failed to notice the light was almost out. And at Girdle Ness the keepers were so dissatisfied with the unproductive state of their gardens that they sent a profit and loss account to the Board.

On the Isle of May that year, work began in June on the installation of the carbon-arc electric light. Because the number of keepers had to be doubled, new houses were being built along with an engine house, a boiler house, a coal store and a workshop, but in October 1886 a report was received from Peter Taylor, farmer of Lochend, Edinburgh, indicating that the island suffered from having been overstocked. Thus there was the vexing question of how the May was going to be able to support the men and their families, for in addition to all their other concerns, the Board, not for the first time in its history, was suffering a considerable financial crisis, not least because of a reduction in light dues ordered by the Board of Trade.

As well as the work going ahead on Ailsa Craig and the Isle of May lights, there was work afoot too on Fidra, the Mull of Kintyre and at Oxcars. Much experimental work was being done on fog signals; a fog signal committee was formed, and the post of fog signal inspector created. It was also generally agreed by the Board that the number of lighthouse stations had quite simply become too large for the two District Superintendents, Muirhead and Dick. The coast was therefore divided into three and an extra superintendent appointed.

And the Board were very keen, even in their financial straits, to add more lights to their list. They applied to Trinity House for nautical sanction for a light on Fair Isle. They received a deputation seeking lights in Oban Bay. They were considering further measures for safety at the southern entrance to the Firth of Forth. The Fair Isle light was sanctioned, and by the year's end the Board were back at Trinity House for sanction to a light at Tarbat Ness.

This bustle of Board activity, the assured and astute approach to their duties, the large empire of lights under their care, would have, quite simply, astounded the founding Commissioners. When they sat down to work out how to build four lights, they could have had little idea that they were sowing the seeds of a complex and far-reaching service with responsibilities, within a century's span, for 72 major lighthouses; many, many minor lights; dozens of buoys and markers; the lighting of wrecks; the setting up of fog signals; and the supervision of warning lights on other waterway obstacles such as the Tay and Forth rail bridges, both abuilding in 1886.

The original Commissioners would, however, have been gratified to note that despite changes wrought on the Board by successive Acts of Parliament, it was, in principle, still the organization of their creation — set up to build lights where they were needed to make the seas more safe, with no consideration of revenue-earning potential. And the Board was still headed by the same sterling mix of provosts and sheriffs but with an extensive staff now of lightkeepers, artificers, sailors, and storemen, not to mention administration and office staff.

The powers of the Northern Lighthouse Board had been altered considerably by a series of Acts of Parliament, but the first real change was brought about by the Act of 1836 when Trinity House was given the power to supervise the Commissioners' activities, a power which was to remain until the Merchant Shipping Act of 1979. An Act of 1854 made the Board of Trade in London the supervisory body in the matter of lighthouse finance, the dues being paid into the Mercantile Marine Fund which the Board of Trade, to the dismay of the Commissioners, began to use as a cash source for expenditure unrelated to lighthouses. In 1883 the collection of the dues was taken over entirely by the Board of Trade, although the responsibility

Joseph Hume (1777-1855) by Sir John Graham-Gilbert.

legally remained with the Commissioners. It was not until 1898 that the General Lighthouse Fund was established and the dues returned to the old Scottish way of being devoted entirely to lighthouse affairs.

In the 19th century, Parliamentary attention to lighthouse matters had not been confined to passing enabling Acts. Reports on many relevant subjects were prepared and presented — from the Bell Rock Lighthouse report that led to the special financial arrangements required for its building to a small report on lighthouses and shipwrecks in the Solway Firth. It was general concern over financial and administrative matters that gave rise to the Select Committee Reports presented in 1834 and 1845, both Committees sitting under the chairmanship of Joseph Hume, the colza-oil enthusiast.

There had been in the early 1820s considerable Parliamentary concern over the large debts incurred by the Commissioners, and in 1830 the Treasury had stepped in to demand that the £55,000 the Commissioners had borrowed in connection with building the Bell Rock Lighthouse and buying the Isle of May be repaid before they launched themselves into any new building. This stricture effectively put a stop to any new lighthouse building for almost ten years.

Joseph Hume, who was known to enjoy his soubriquet, 'the apostle of thrift', was the son of a Montrose sea captain and would have been well aware of the work of the Northern Lighthouse Board. The representatives of the Board before the Committee were the Secretary, Charles Cuningham, the Engineer, Robert Stevenson, and his son Alan, who had lately become his father's partner, having been his assistant, and James Maconochie, Sheriff of Orkney. The hundreds of questions put to them ranged from the manner in which they went about scientific enquiry to how the George Street office was run. The Commissioners in their earlier years had held their meetings at various venues, but the special committees had usually met at the Secretary's home, from which all the actual correspondence was done. Then, in 1829, premises were acquired at 84 George Street in the New Town of Edinburgh, with the Stevensons' office on the third floor and a fine courtyard and stables at the rear of the building, convenient for experimental work with the lamps.

What Joseph Hume's 1834 Committee principally revealed were the very great differences that existed between the management of the three lighthouse services in England, Scotland and Ireland. This and the 1845 Report demonstrated certain administrative and technological superiorities in the Scottish service, but Hume concluded that it might be best to create a new overall lighthouse authority laying down uniformity of practice throughout the British Isles. He was overruled by his Committee who, instead, made Trinity House the final British arbiter in lighthouse matters.

After the Merchant Shipping Act of 1854 and the involvement of the Board of Trade, the Commissioners felt increasingly aggrieved by what they often justifiably deemed unjustifiable interference from London. The cost of the building of Scottish lighthouses was brought into question again and again, with concomitant delay and frustration. The chief source of irritation seems often to have been an implied English belief that because they had more shipping using their ports, then it was English money that was the principal contributor to the fund. Further, there was also the implication in much of a voluminous three-way correspondence that built up between Trinity House, the Board of Trade and 84 George Street that the cost of building lights had less to do with the unavoidable extra cost of putting up lights in locations and conditions unknown on English coasts than with the determined profligacy of the Commissioners!

Enforced economies gave rise to the substitution of brick for stone in Scottish lighthouse building and often quite unsuitable slate roofing in place of lead. Any Commissioners' attempts to contradict the opinions of southern engineers, ignorant of Scottish conditions, were more than a little hampered by the Board of Trade's refusal, for a time, from 1854 to allow the Commissioners an Engineer as part of their establishment. The Northern Lighthouse Board could call upon the Stevensons as occasional consultants but not have them in regular attendance at committee and Board meetings nor as on-site engineers. After prolonged protest, the Board of Trade relented.

Despite all this interference, however, the Commissioners retained a firm grip on the actual day-to-day running of their service in Scotland. The care and the quality of the lights and the men of the lights remained their abiding and principal concern, even when it might mean missing an opportunity to draw international attention to their fine work. One such incident was when they planned to send apparatus by *Pharos* to the Paris Exhibition of 1867. The trip was abandoned when it was realized that the ship was urgently needed to take equipment to the Auskerry lighthouse which was nearing completion. Happily, at the last minute it was discovered that they could send their exhibit on a regular Leith to Dunkirk ship, and then by road to Paris just in time for the Exhibition.

THE VOYAGE

Until the Board of Trade's refusal to allow them their Engineer, the Commissioners had been largely dependent on the annual Engineer's Report to bring them up to date with the state of their lights and the keepers. But gradually, since around 1814, a tradition had grown up of Commissioners accompanying the Engineer on his rounds to see for themselves the extent and condition of their domain, and by the 1850s the Commissioners' voyage had become an annual event.

These voyages were far more than the social junket they were often suspected of being. Commissioners took the opportunity not only of visiting and inspecting the condition of the houses and the lights but of listening to grievances from the keepers, meeting the local people on whose goodwill and practical help the keepers often depended, and, above all, of seeing at first hand the difficulties and dangers keepers endured, particularly in getting to and from the rock towers.
No notice was given to the keepers that the Commissioners were on their way, a tradition maintained until comparatively recent times.

On 21 July 1886 at three o'clock in the afternoon, *Pharos* sailed from Granton on the Commissioners' Voyage, with James Pringle, Provost of Leith, James Murdoch, the Board's Cashier who became General Manager in 1892, F.A. Forbes of London, a cousin of Mr Pringle, and George Clark, son of the Lord Provost of Edinburgh, on board.

First, *Pharos* steamed up to the new Oxcars light on the Fife side of the estuary and then proceeded to Queensferry to view the building work on the new Forth Bridge. At Inchkeith they discovered that the keepers and families had had no occasion to call the doctor for a year, and since the doctor was being paid a retainer for his services, it was mooted that the least he could do for his money would be to visit the island once a year to give everyone a health check. Professor Madigan's Report would still have been fresh in their minds. Moving down the estuary, they found Fidra's gardens untidy, St Abb's Head gardens in good order, and on the Isle of May they took a look at the engines being assembled for the electric lighting. The crops looked good — an erroneous impression, as Mr Taylor's report would point out.

Turning north, their next stop was Arbroath where they met Principal Lightkeeper Jack and the Third Assistant, Mr Cadger, at the Signal Tower. This Mr Cadger, James Cadger, was destined one day to be the Master of the service vessel *Pole Star*, and his three sons would follow him into the service, two as eventual superintendents and one as a lightkeeper. Since a landing at the Bell Rock was impossible because of high seas, the *Pharos* proceeded on to Montroseness, where they found the Principal Lightkeeper very ill indeed. What was worse, he had not been able to send for his occasional keeper from Ferryden as typhoid was raging in the village. An urgent letter was promptly despatched to 84 George Street, asking that 'Jolly, an assistant storekeeper trained for such an emergency' be sent to Montrose with all speed. Despite the condition of the poor PLK, all was found to be in good order, as was Girdle Ness.

At Aberdeen, the party was joined by Norman Macpherson, Sheriff of Dumfries, Thomas Clark, Lord Provost of Edinburgh, and Aeneas Mackay, Sheriff of Fife. The weather had turned foggy and wet. The PLK at Buchan Ness was in bed with inflammation of the knee when they called; the lighthouse was, however, in good order. Next stop was Chanonry Point, at the entrance to the Inner Moray Firth, bad weather having prevented landings at Kinnaird Head and at Covesea Skerries. At Chanonry there turned out to be a whole thirty-minute difference between local and Greenwich time. It was decided that this was the fault of the sundial which had been wrongly set.

Since a General Order of 29 January 1852, it had been the practice to have clocks set at local time calculated from sundial readings. The order is precise: 'The Lighthouse Timepiece is to be kept right, by observing, if possible, once a week, the indication of the Sun-dial, in the following manner:- The Principal Keeper shall go to the dial, when the sun is shining, and shall watch until the shadow of the style touches any hour, half hour or other time agreed upon beforehand with the Assistant, who shall stand on the balcony, waiting a signal from the Principal. The Principal shall then make the signal, on seeing which, the Assistant shall immediately set the Timepiece to the time already agreed upon. The Principal shall then take a note from the Table of the Equation of Time engraved on the Sun-dial, of the number of minutes by which the clock should differ from the time given by the dial; and shall afterwards proceed at once to the Lightroom where he shall put the timepiece back or forward according as the Clock shall be slower or faster than the Sun at the time.'

After visiting Cromarty and finding it in good order, bad weather forced *Pharos* to put in to Invergordon and remain there until the weather cleared on 28 July. Tarbat Ness light was visited before breakfast on that day, and then the Commissioners proceeded north.

Next stop was Dunnet Head on the Pentland Firth. Due note was taken that the crops had suffered badly in the recent stormy weather. Here, as at Scrabster and Holburn Head, and later at Cantick Head, the visitors were plainly impressed by the spotless state of the keepers'

Captain James Cadger.

48

dwelling houses — 'patterns of neatness'. PLK and Mrs Charleson from Cantick Head were taken on board the *Pharos* to Kirkwall to catch a steamer for the south, where they were to take a short holiday.

Bad weather, east winds, high seas and then fog now dogged the progress of the vessel, which was unable to land the voyagers at Pentland Skerries, nor at Start Point, nor North Ronaldsay. *Pharos* proceeded to Bressay via Auskerry and then to Sumburgh Head, with a good view of Fair Isle en route. In fog they crept into Bressay at 1p.m., where they found the clock stopped at 11 — the keepers had probably not seen them coming!

At Lerwick they were joined by John Cheyne, Sheriff of Ross, and after calling at Bressay Sound and Whalsey they headed north to Muckle Flugga, their most northerly outpost, only to find they could not land because of heavy seas. Instead, they anchored in Burrafirth and inspected the houses at the Muckle Flugga Shore Station, discovering there were, in fact, no married men amongst the keepers. One keeper made bold enough to say he was 'quite ready to marry, but his intended, living in Dundee, could not be brought to such an out of the way place to commence her married life'. Perhaps, if they could move him to a less isolated place for a time, he suggested, he would have no objection to going back to a rock station afterwards. When the gilt was off the marital gingerbread, no doubt!

And so the voyage continued, the weather turning for the better for a time as *Pharos* headed south. At North Ronaldsay and Start Point there were new wrecks to inspect as well as PLK Dawson's lately ruined garden at Pentland Skerries. Garden damage was seen, too, at Hoy High and Hoy Low. Comrie Thomson, Sheriff of Forfar, joined the party at Scrabster, and *Pharos* sailed west to Cape Wrath where the keepers were caught completely unawares. PLK Morrison was in the lightroom, but the light reflectors were not as clean as they ought to have been, and it was evident the brasses and lamp glass had not been cleaned that morning. As if that were not enough, the lightroom clock was a whole hour behind Greenwich time — again a faulty sundial, the PLK claimed. Nor were the houses particularly tidy. With some compassion, the Commissioners realized poor Morrison's house was probably unkempt because his wife had only lately died, but at the Assistant's house, although he was married they were greeted by a servant girl and only later was it explained to them that the ALK's wife had actually been in the house, in a box bed with her baby. After this inspection, the Commissioners asked that a letter be sent to PLK Morrison pointing out their dissatisfaction with what they had found.

The next port of call was Monach, where the keeper informed them that he had not seen half a dozen vessels of any sort in a year. En route to Oban, the Sound of Mull light was inspected before *Pharos* ended her voyage at Oban on 10 August, conveniently in time to let the gentlemen on board head for the moors for the Glorious Twelfth.

In the entire account in the 1886 Minute Book of this voyage, there is not a single mention of the centenary or of any celebration attending upon it. There is no hint that the voyage was a momentous one in any way. Indeed, the report is a matter-of-fact account of duty done despite adverse weather. For the day on which they might have celebrated, there is this entry: '1st August. Sunday — Lerwick Harbour'. Perhaps they spent it quietly contemplating one hundred years of achievement. Perhaps they gave prayerful thanks for the work so far. Perhaps they just forgot.

Sundial on the Isle of May.

STEADY AHEAD

The Commissioners of the Northern Lighthouses began their work in 1786 with no real means to hand of achieving the purpose of their Trust, but by the end of their first century their service had become one of the two acknowledged leaders in the field. In his *Report of a Tour of Inspection of European Light-House Systems Made in 1873*, Major George H. Elliot of the Corps of Engineers of the United States Army and member and Engineer-Secretary of the Lighthouse Board of America, describes for the Senate the Northern Lighthouse Board: 'The committees of the Board meet twice a month, but the entire executive functions are exercised by the secretary and engineers. The latter are Messrs David and Thomas Stevenson, whose published writings on lighthouses and their illumination have not only given them a worldwide fame, but have established the reputation of the lighthouse system of Scotland as second to none but that of France, which is acknowledged to be the model for all others.

'Both were unfortunately absent the first morning I called, and I took the opportunity of seeing somewhat of Edinburgh, which, I think, is justly called the most picturesque city of Europe.'

Happily the Major did meet up with the Stevensons in the end and included in his report not only glowing tributes to the Board's engineers but an assessment of the excellence of Young's Scottish 'paraffine', which he notes the NLB had not been immediately allowed to adopt on the orders of the Board of Trade acting under the advice of Trinity House.

The fame of the NLB and of the Stevensons was truly worldwide. As early as 1861 the Stevenson firm had been asked to design a light for a lighthouse off the coast of Burma and within five years they had supplied nine lights for nine eastern locations from Aden to Sumatra. The bulk of the equipment required, as well as the expertise for installing the lights, came from Scotland. It was, for instance, a Montrose man with lighthouse connections who went to Egypt to be lighthouse master there when the Suez Canal was being built.

But from the end of the 19th century onwards, although the Northern Lighthouse Board's engineers were to remain in the forefront of lamp technology and of building techniques, the means of changing the entire character of the service came from outside sources, and by 1886 some of these were already in existence.

In 1874, Alexander Graham Bell, born in Edinburgh but working in the United States, invented a practical telephone, and within a few years telephone exchanges were being opened up all over Britain. It is believed that the first telephone used in Scotland was the shore to diver phone connected up during the salvage operations after the Tay Rail Bridge disaster of 1879. Telephone technicians had been in Dundee preparing for the opening in the city on 10 January 1880 of the first exchange. This was quickly followed by the establishment of exchanges in Edinburgh and Glasgow. Soon after, the first submarine telephone cable in Britain was laid across the River Tay from Dundee, to link a single subscriber in Fife to the fast-growing system.

The success of that cable did not escape the attention of the NLB. A telegraph service dependent on Morse signalling had been in operation in Britain for many years, but as the Post Office established its telephone service network it began to offer a fast and efficient telegram service, and lighthouses within a reasonable distance of a post office

Model (one-fifth actual size) of a Stevenson lighting apparatus made for a lighthouse in Singapore.

now had a fast means of sending urgent messages to headquarters. In many places for some time to come, however, there was to be no alternative to the old signalling methods. At Ailsa Craig, a fire beacon was lit if the attendance of a doctor was urgently required. Otherwise messages were sent over to Girvan on the Ayrshire coast by carrier pigeon. At other remote stations the sole possibility of summoning help was, in daylight, a complex relay system of flag signals hoisted at lookout points, or at night by firing distress flares, both depending for effectiveness on alert watchers and clear weather.

The signal tower at Hynish relayed messages from Earraid to Dubh Artach. Between Skerryvore and Earraid it was possible to signal directly by heliograph — weather permitting. A day of passing clouds could be nothing short of exasperating, as on the occasion when Earraid began to flash a message to the Principal Keeper at Skerryvore, whose wife was something of a hypochondriac. The message began well enough, 'Mrs So-and-so has got. . . .' Across scudded clouds, and the PLK, imagining all sorts of ailments afflicting his poor wife, had to wait some time before he learned that what his wife had got was 'a goose in the Christmas raffle'!

How much easier were things for the Keeper at Callanish who could telegraph to George Street, 'Steamer Kitty distress for coals will I supply three ton to take them to Stornoway'. The instant reply — 'Telegram received. You may supply steamer with three tons of coal. Owners will be charged cost price.'

If it is the case that Guglielmo Marconi was inspired in his work on radio transmission by the thought that by radio the lighthouse men would be put in contact with the outside world and thus 'render their isolation less painful', he was not alone in grasping the enormous importance radio contact could have in the running of the lighthouse service. David A. Stevenson, Engineer to the Board in 1895, had considered installing a wireless telegraphy link from Lewis to the Flannans when the lighthouse was begun there at the end of the 19th century. In fact, an experimental wireless telephone service was set up at the Flannans in 1907. The success of this encouraged the Board to install other wireless communication links with very isolated places, and as the landline telephone system grew, phones, too, were increasingly installed where possible, or some arrangement made to pass telephone messages from the nearest phone to the lighthouse.

The limited technology of the early years of this century necessitated, at times, some fairly complicated arrangements as, for instance, in 1912 for the newly built Rubh' Re light. A telephone link was established between Strath on Gairloch and Inverasdale on Loch Ewe and the lighthouse 'for lifesaving purposes. It has also been arranged to have a branch call to Melvaig for keepers to call in the Occasional when necessary.' Kenneth Macrae, the shopkeeper at Melvaig, was paid £4 per annum for taking these calls and passing them on to the Occasional.

The installation of telephones continued during the First World War, but sometimes when the Navy had installed a phone at a shore station for its own benefit, wrangles blew up between the NLB and the Admiralty over allowing the keepers use of these phones in emergencies.

Gradually, as the technology of communication improved, more and more of the isolated stations and rock stations were connected to shore by radio telephone, but even as late as the 1930s at Out Skerries,

Rubh' Re Lighthouse.

Morse and semaphore were the only communication between the lighthouse and the shore station, all of three-quarters of a mile away.

Today every lighthouse is linked to headquarters by a direct radio telephone system connecting 84 George Street not only with the lights but with the lighthouse tenders and the stores, and the offshore stations not only have radio-telephone links but are linked to the national telephone system.

Guglielmo Marconi's work was destined to help the lightkeeper and ameliorate his sense of isolation in quite another way, when national broadcasting began in Britain in the 1920s. The men of the lights who had often to wait many weeks for news of the outside world were quick to rig cat's-whisker sets and tune in, although their efforts were often frustrated by the frailty of aerials which tended to disappear in gales. Fifty years on, many listeners in the towers turned into broadcasters in their own right — over Citizens' Band radio. Today, television helps to while away off-duty hours, although a choice of channels can sometimes be the source of friction in the towers!

THE LATER LIGHTS

From Kinnaird Head in 1787 to Oxcars in 1886, the Commissioners of Northern Lighthouses built 68 manned lighthouses. In the years from 1887 to 1969, when they built the last manned station at the Calf of Man, they had constructed 25 lighthouses and the manned North Carr lightvessel. Among the lights to go up in those latter 82 years were some whose building represents the finest achievements of the service — Fair Isle (South and North) in 1892, Sule Skerry in 1895, Flannan Islands in 1899 and Hyskeir in 1904.

Sule Skerry lies forty miles west of Orkney and about fifty north of Cape Wrath and remains the most remote of all lighthouses in the British Isles. Even with the mechanical equipment available to the engineers and builders in the 1890s, it took two seasons to build the lighthouse — an 88-foot tower with a very large lantern. So powerful was the light, thanks to a lens arrangement devised by Charles Stevenson, that it could, in fact, be seen at Cape Wrath.

Hyskeir is a tiny islet in the Inner Hebrides, west of Rhum and southwest of Canna, and just the kind of place which, one hundred years before, the Commissioners would have had little hesitation in establishing as a family station, with the men and their families living off the ten acres of relatively good land. But when the light was lit in 1904, the Shore Station was established at Oban and the families settled into the community with its good schooling and other amenities.

This policy of housing the families within existing communities on shore and not simply at the nearest convenient landfall to the light was one increasingly pursued by the Commissioners. When, in 1899, they built the Flannan Isles Shore Station at Breasclete, Loch Roag, Lewis, the situation of the houses was isolated enough, and yet no more so than the crofting community around. It was into this station that the first Flannan Isles keepers' families moved, including those of PLK James Ducat and Assistants Thomas Marshall, William Ross and Joseph Moore. Donald MacArthur was appointed the first Occasional Keeper at the new rock station.

The Flannan Isles are a scattering of islands lying fifteen miles west of Lewis. It was on the largest of the Flannans, Eilean Mor, that the

A horse being hoisted up to the lighthouse workings on Eilean Mor in the Flannan Islands.

lighthouse was built, in a remarkable exercise even by NLB standards. Everything required to build and store the light had to be taken up 150-foot-high cliffs. Landing places were created on both the east and west sides of the island, each with near-vertical stepped paths hewn out of the rock face and leading upwards to the grassy plateau on which the light tower was built.

Despite the awesome approaches, which are incredibly hazardous in bad weather, the Flannan Lighthouse inspired a great affection in the keepers who manned the light until it was automated in 1971. The islands were reputedly very healthy places, and more than one keeper claimed that colds caught on leave quickly vanished out on Eilean Mor. Sheep were taken out to the island to graze until their mutton was required, and it was a popular place of call for foreign fishermen anxious to supplement their diet with freshly shot rabbit or a bit of salty mutton in exchange for fish.

On fine, balmy days Eilean Mor is an enchanting place. On winters' days, the seas surge up and engulf the landing places with power and height enough to sweep away anything not securely anchored to the slithery rock. This terrible and always sudden mountain of water is a phenomenon that was perhaps unknown to Keepers Ducat and Marshall and Occasional Keeper MacArthur, who had joined them on duty on 7 December 1900, at the regular fortnightly relief.

The next relief day at the Flannans was 26 December, when Joseph Moore, the Assistant, was picked up by the lighthouse tender *Hesperus* to be taken out to the rock. Because of the landing difficulties, there was a pre-arranged flag signal system to indicate to approaching ships which landing would be the better and safer on a particular day or whether no landing at all should be attempted. That 26 December there was no flag of any kind to be seen as the *Hesperus* approached. Captain Harvie of *Hesperus* blew the steam whistle and sounded the boat's siren and then fired a rocket. None of these actions provoked any kind of response from the island, so the boat was lowered and Joseph Moore was rowed ashore to the east landing.

Later that day a telegram from Captain Harvie arrived at 84 George Street: 'A dreadful accident has happened at Flannans. The three Keepers, Ducat, Marshall and the Occasional have disappeared from the Island. On our arrival there this afternoon no signs of life was to be seen on the Island. Fired a rocket but, as no response was made, managed to land Moore who went up to the station but found no Keepers there. The clocks were stopped and other signs indicated that the accident must have happened about a week ago. Poor fellows they must have been blown over the cliffs or drowned trying to secure a crane or something like that. Night coming on, we could not wait to make further investigation but will go off again tomorrow morning to try and learn something as to their fate. I have left Moore, Macdonald, Buoymaster and two seamen on the Island to keep the light burning until you make other arrangements. Will not return to Oban until I hear from you. I have repeated this wire to Muirhead, in case you are not at home. I will remain at the telegraph office tonight until it closes, if you wish to wire me.'

Two days later, Joseph Moore, the Assistant Keeper, set down his version of events: 'I was the first to land leaving Mr McCormack and his men in the boat till I should return from the lighthouse. I went up, and on coming to the entrance gate I found it closed. I made for the entrance door leading to the kitchen and store room, and found it also closed and the door inside that, but the kitchen door itself was open. On entering the kitchen I looked at the fireplace and saw that the fire was not lighted for some days. I then entered the rooms in succession, found the beds empty just as they left them in the early morning. I did not take time to search further, for I only too well knew that something serious had occurred. I darted out and made for the landing. When I reached there I informed Mr McCormack that the place was deserted. He with some of the men came up a second time, so as to make sure, but unfortunately the first impression was only too true. Mr McCormack and myself proceeded to the lightroom where every thing was left in proper order. The lamp was cleaned, the fountain full, blinds on the windows etc. We left and proceeded on board the steamer. On arrival Captain Harvey ordered me back again to the Island accompanied with Mr McDonald (Buoymaster), A. Campbell and A. Lamont who were to do duty with me till timely aid should arrive. We went on shore and proceeded up to the lightroom and lighted the light in the proper time that night and every night since. The following day we traversed the Island from end to end but still nothing to be seen to convince us how it happened. Nothing appears touched at East Landing to show that they were taken from there. Ropes are all in their respective places in the shelter, just as they were left after the relief on 7th. On West side it is somewhat different. We had an old box halfway up the railway for holding West Landing mooring ropes and tackle, and it has gone. Some of the ropes it appears got washed out of it; they lie strewn on the rocks near the crane. The crane itself is safe.

'From the Monthly Return it is evident they are missing since 15th. Up till 13th is marked in the book and 14th is marked on slate along with part of 15th. On 14th the prevailing state of the weather was: Westerly Stg Brz Shrs [strong breeze, showers]. On 15th the hour of extinguishing was noted on slate along with barometer and thermometer inside and outside lantern, taken at 9 a.m. as usual, and direction of wind. The kitchen utensils were all very clean, which is a sign it must have been after dinner some time they left. There is one thing I know that Mr Marshall never wore seaboots, or oilskins, only when in connection with landing.'

Poor Joseph Moore. He had been the first to search the deserted tower, the first to realize his colleagues and friends, close companions and family men, had vanished. It is little wonder that in a report made by Mr Muirhead, the Superintendent, some days later, Moore was noted to be in a nervous state, and Lamont, the seaman from *Hesperus*, had been ordered to keep him company on lightroom duty for the succeeding week or two. Muirhead was sympathetic enough to suggest that 'if this nervousness does not leave Moore, he will require to be transferred, but I am reluctant to recommend this, as I would desire to have one man at least who knows the work of the Station'.

Later reports, in particular from the master of a steamer which had passed near to the Flannans on the night of the 15th, confirmed that indeed the light had not shown that night.

The Superintendent's examination of the circumstances and of the west landing led him to this conclusion and explanation of what had occurred: 'After a careful examination of the place, the railings, ropes, etc, and weighing all the evidence which I could secure, I am of opinion that the most likely explanation of the disappearance of the men is that they had all gone down on the afternoon of Saturday

15 December to the proximity of the West landing, to secure the box with the mooring ropes etc and that an unexpectedly large roller had come up on the Island, and a large body of water being up higher than where they were and coming down upon them had swept them away with resistless force.' That large body of water was a feature of Flannan Islands' conditions and became known to every keeper who ever served on that station — the sudden sea that came rushing and clasping at men going about their ordinary duties.

The story of the disappearance of the Keepers in 1900 was immortalized in a poem written some years later by Wilfred Wilson Gibson, entitled 'Flannan Isle', and the tale of the lost Scottish lightkeepers entered the lexicon of mystery tales that are told the world over. And Mr Muirhead was left wondering if it would not have been better to have equipped the Flannans with a wireless telegraph system from the very start.

Thirty-six years later, at Monach, another tragedy occurred to underline once more to the general public the fact that the men of the lights confront daily dangers — and even with a radio-telephone to summon help. Robert Williamson, who was First Mate of the Northern Lighthouse tender *Pole Star* from 1936 to 1939 and later Master, told his story in the Northern Lighthouse Journal of the Monach Keepers who vanished one stormy November night: 'On 15th November 1936 during a severe spell of winter weather J.W. Milne, PLK, and W. Black, ALK [there were only two keepers at the lighthouse] had decided to go for the overdue mail and provisions, which meant crossing the Sound, about 100 yards, in their dinghy, and a walk over the rough sandy wire grass covering Heisker Island to the place where the Attending Boatmen left the goods which he brought from Bayhead, North Uist. They were seen to load the dinghy at the ferry slipway, push off and row for Monach Island but by now the weather had deteriorated with strong crosswinds and hail showers, together with strong through going tides which were rising and which beat them off and prevented them making progress. Desperately they struggled on but time and tide and the weather had sapped their now-failing strength and it was only by a supreme effort that they managed to reach a flat-shaped submerged rock just outside line-throwing distance of the slipway. Suddenly, as if mercifully sent, a very heavy hail and snow shower obliterated the grim scene and both men had disappeared without trace.'

The Principal's sister, alone, manned the Monach light that night, trying again and again to contact whoever might be listening on the radio-telephone. How much longer Miss Milne might have had to wait for help had it not been for that radio link it is impossible to say, but the loss of the Monach men dispelled any notion that modern technology made a rock keeper's life any safer. The elements are so often a bitter enemy. And it has long been conjectured that the only possible way of not risking men's lives in lighthouse keeping is not to have men at the lighthouses at all. In the second half of the 20th century, conjecture is now a fact.

In the 1950s, the lighthouses at both Chicken Rock and Skerryvore were severely damaged by fire. Mercifully, in neither case were lives lost, but the damage at Skerryvore was such that it was four years before men came back to man a light here. In the interim, an automatic Dalen light was placed on the rock, and the reliability of this Swedish light pointed the way clear ahead for future automation. Chicken

Rock, which had been built to take over from the Calf of Man in 1875, was also automated in 1962.

In 1958, at Strathy Point, between Dunnet Head and Cape Wrath, Senior Commissioner Sir Robert Maconochie inaugurated the new lighthouse. The Commissioners had chivvied Trinity House and the Board of Trade since 1903 for permission to build this light, which after it was finally permitted in 1953 ended up costing one hundred times more than the original estimate.

Strathy, with its electric light, precast concrete and brick structure, its modern houses, its nearby school, will probably be the last manned lighthouse built in Scotland. The Calf of Man light, built in 1969, will have the distinction, no doubt, of being the last manned lighthouse ever built by the Northern Lighthouse Board. And its construction marked another momentous development in the service.

At the Calf of Man the light is linked to the landing place by a mile of narrow track. To overcome this difficulty, it was decided to design a lighthouse none of whose component parts would weigh more than a quarter tonne and to fly all of these parts in to the site by helicopter. Over 960 tonnes were thus landed over about six weeks, and the entire Calf of Man station — engine room, keepers' quarters, the tower, the light, and so on — were completed in one summer building season. Fuel is pumped across country to the light so the building of a substantial road was unnecessary. How Robert and Alan Stevenson would have loved the simple practicality of it all!

Since the discovery of oil in the North Sea in the 1960s, the new traffic in these waters has necessitated the building of a number of new beacons and lights, particularly around the vast new oil terminal at Sullom Voe in Shetland. Bases for the beacons were prepared on site, but the actual structures of glass-reinforced plastic were flown in by large helicopter. The technique and the material have proved so successful that steel-framed buildings clad with glass-reinforced plastic panels are now used for engine rooms and accommodation for maintenance personnel at several stations.

Prefabrication to minimize work time on site was precisely what Robert Stevenson pioneered when he set up that stone yard in Arbroath to hew the heavy stones that were to provide the deadweight that anchors his Bell Rock Lighthouse to its watery shelf. This heavy-base principle was retained by his successors in their tower lights, such as Skerryvore and Dubh Artach. Today that deadweight in rock towers is provided — as at the superb Ve Skerries light of 1977 — by drilling three to four metres down into the bedrock and setting into the rock large-diameter high-tensile steel bars. These are then extended upwards to the top of the tower by lifts and post-tensioned by hydraulic jacks. The result at Ve Skerries produced a downward force amounting to well over 1,800 tonnes and a solid, strong tower.

In 1986 the northern and western passages around Scotland are still those which greatly exercise the Commissioners and their engineers. In Yell Sound, three new lights have been set up to help oil tankers through to the Sullom Voe Terminal, and the Shetland Fishermen and Lerwick Harbour Trust have only in recent years requested a light on Hoo Stack, athwart the eastern approaches to Lerwick. So the work continues, and a latterday George Dempster might be forgiven for likening our coasts today more to Piccadilly Circus than to Pall Mall, for despite the plethora of sophisticated shipboard computerized direction-finding equipment, the mariner still looks for the comforting light.

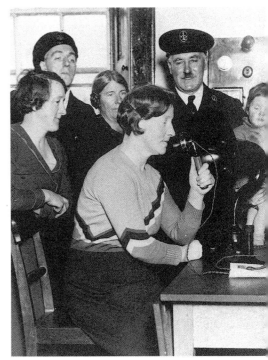

The wife of a keeper talking in January 1934 to her husband imprisoned by bad weather in the Dubh Artach Lighthouse. One of the keepers, Thomas Budge, injured a leg and it was several days before he could be rescued.

56

TECHNOLOGY AND TENDERS

Automation and the demanning of the lights has become possible only because of the extraordinary technological advances of recent times, most of them made for application in other fields and then adapted to the lighthouse purpose. Amongst these are radar, solar panels and automatic monitoring.

In the 19th century, the limited brilliance of light sources gave rise to some quite remarkable and very effective arrangements of lenses and prisms in order to achieve maximum candlepower. When higher wattage electric lamps became available, it was found that the large arrangements of lenses were comparatively ineffectual in reflecting from such a small surface source. Smaller lens arrangements were therefore devised — some of them as small as two feet in diameter — to replace the 10-foot-high by 6-foot-diameter lenses which had in their era been the marvel of the service. (The carbon-arc May light proved to be so manpower-intensive that it was reconverted to oil in 1919 and then later to ordinary electricity.)

The cost of creating even the smaller lenses for use with electricity became almost prohibitive in the 1930s and 40s, and at that time mirror systems, which had been developed during the First World War for the earliest searchlights, provided a solution to light-intensification problems. It is curious that after all the long years of experiment with lights and lenses, the arrangements of prisms that so absorbed the Fresnels and the Stevensons, the lighting engineers returned in the end to mirrors — Thomas Smith's original solution. Today's new power source is the sun — solar panels collecting and storing enough

Top: Pharos *and* Fingal *at the lighthouse pier in Oban. Above: A cardinal buoy being hoisted on board* Pharos *for overhaul.*

electricity to fuel and revolve the powerful new lights, sealed-beam lamps which resemble nothing so much as rows of car headlights mounted on a revolving framework.

The discovery of North Sea oil has not just involved the NLB in the provision of major lights and beacons in the Shetlands and Orkneys; it has meant, too, the inspection of the warning lights on oil-exploration rigs and platforms. And the development of formerly nearly abandoned fishing harbours in the north and along the east coast as offshore supply depots has also added a considerable volume of work in the laying of lit and unlit buoys.

At the end of the 19th century many buoys were gas-filled. The NLB had its own gas installations at Granton, Stromness and Oban, and from these depots the gas was pumped into a gas barge and then shipped out to the buoys. The early gas buoys had an open flame and a fixed light, incandescent mantles and flashing mechanisms not coming into use until the early 1950s. Dissolved acetylene gas replaced coal gas in the 1930s, and the old gas installations at the three ports were dismantled. Acetylene is still used today, principally because it is reliable and requires little maintenance. Batteries, too, are used and recharged annually, and now solar panels are proving their value as a constant power source. In fact, it was the successful experimentation with solar panels on fixed lights and buoys that encouraged the engineers to experiment with them for the major lights, and when the Bell Rock is demanned in 1987 the power source for rotating the lens of the automatic acetylene light will be the sun.

Automation doesn't stop at lights and beacons. Today, automatic fog detectors are used to start and stop fog signals in both manned and unmanned stations. The signals themselves are now either sirens or compressed-air diaphones, and some of the fog signals are triggered by radio control from stations some distance away.

Buoy maintenance being carried out off Barra.

Remote control, radio and radar together have revolutionized the work of lightkeepers and mariners alike in this century. The use of radio, not only for communication but for signalling and giving bearings, was developed early in the century, and in 1927 at Kinnaird Head the NLB installed its first radio beacon. Radio beacons operate on a medium frequency and transmit a coded signal which gives a bearing on the station. By picking up two or three station signals, a ship can easily pinpoint its exact position, and these signals are being modified to transmit other information to mariners.

Radar beacons (racons) on lighthouses and buoys have been installed in considerable numbers in more recent years. Triggered by radar on board ship, the signals emitted by the racons are displayed on ships' radar screens, giving a range and bearing from the lighthouse or buoy. These are unfailing signals even in the worst, foggiest conditions.

Even the needs of the weekend pleasure sailor and the fisherman have not been overlooked in all this sophistication. None of their craft is expected in the foreseeable future to carry much more than relatively rudimentary navigational aids. Not for them the joys of radar nor of satellite weather reports. And even if the pleasure yachtsman pays no dues to the Board — and probably does not even realize that none of the lights he finds along his way costs the taxpayer a penny — the NLB has recently been evaluating for his benefit a radio lighthouse system whereby all that will be required in the way of equipment on board will be a VHF radio set to receive the bleepy signals.

As the lights are automated and the needs of the service change, it is inevitable that the role of the Commissioners' ships will change too. One hundred years ago, the little fleet comprised the fifth *Pharos,* the SS *Signal,* built in 1883, based at Oban and sadly wrecked in 1895 on the Mull of Kintyre while sailing from Greenock back to her home base. The first *Pole Star,* a steel, twin-screw steamer, was launched in 1892 and based at Stromness. This stout little ship served for almost forty years before giving way to the second *Pole Star* in Stromness in 1930. *Pole Star* the third was completed in 1961, and, with a helicopter pad on her afterdeck, is currently the tender based at Stromness.

There have been two Oban-based ships called *Hesperus* in the service, the first commissioned in 1896 and the second in 1939. The latter's place as the Oban tender was taken by the *Fingal* in 1963, and *Hesperus* ended her days as the oil-rig tender *Sperus.*

The series of storing ships called *May* began in 1899, and although *May* one and two were launched with the name, *May* three was *May* two renamed, while *May* four was *Pole Star* the second renamed — just the kind of ploy that keeps marine historians happily diverted for hours in later years!

Pharos number six was the fleet's flagship for forty-six years, before being replaced by the present *Pharos* in 1955. Based at Granton, this quite splendid steel, twin-screw motor vessel is the commodore ship of the flotilla, and as well as taking the Commissioners on their annual round, it serves as the normal tender for the Bell Rock, Isle of May and Bass Rock lighthouses as well as maintaining the buoys in the area. Until recent times, all transfers and storing were done by tender. Today stations on shore are 'stored' by road whenever possible.

In both World Wars, the ships and the lightvessel *North Carr* saw active service. The *North Carr* took up station in the Clyde and the NLB ships went about their duties with the additional task of marking mine channels. The ships were provided with rifles and then machine guns to shoot at mines. The only weapon of any consequence on board was a 12-pounder gun.

Once upon a time, all fuel landed from the tenders had to be manhauled up to the lights. Today, fuel is either pumped or else hauled by foreloaders or tractors and trailers, which have replaced, too, the horses and donkeys that used to help the keepers at stations including Ushenish, Auskerry and the Isle of May. The Isle of May horse was given up when it transpired that the only thing it was being asked to haul was its own fodder!

But at other stations, particularly the rocks, the main storing power is still manpower. Anyone witnessing a Bell Rock boat relief today — even in as flat a calm as that reef will allow — must be impressed by the amount of courage and knowledge required to bring the little motor launch fast up the gully approach to the grating. For a minute or two there is a great flurry of activity of unloading food and water and other supplies, and loading on to the launch empty containers and the men going ashore. It is only a minute or two — about twenty at the most — that conditions allow the boat to stay. It must be turned about to bounce out of the gully in the ebbing tide.

Family tradition, marriages between lightkeepers' families, and lifelong service are very much a part of the lighthouse story. So, too, are the promotional opportunities that allow men of ability to climb to the top of the service no matter how lowly their first rung. And that particular tradition applies to the men of the tenders as well as those of the lights. One man's story will serve as example for them all.

James W. Hunter was 15 when he joined the steamship *Pharos* in 1919 as cook's boy. Four years later he transferred to the Deck Department as an Ordinary Seaman, and two years later was promoted to Able Seaman. He evidently caught the attention of the famous Captain Ewing of the *Pharos* and, as a likely lad, was advised by the Captain to try to gain Foreign Going Certificates. Only three days later, young Hunter found himself signed up on his first foreign-going vessel, and for the next six years he sailed the oceans on passenger and trading vessels. But his heart was at home with the lighthouse service, and in 1932 he was appointed Second Officer on *Hesperus*, based in Oban. The cook's boy gained his Master's Certificate in 1934, and he served subsequently as Chief Officer on *May*, *Pharos* and *Pole Star*, and in 1955 became Master of *Hesperus* — in his own words 'a tremendous challenge, as this was the biggest area to cover, from Skye to the Isle of Man, with the most rock reliefs in the service'. In 1958, 39 years after he had first joined, he became Master of the commodore vessel *Pharos*. In 1970, James W. Hunter became the Board's first Marine Superintendent.

In his forty-six years of service, Captain Hunter wrote an invaluable book on rock lighthouse landings and theses on the operation of the carbide acetylene foghorn, and in his intimate and exhaustive knowledge of every aspect of the service in his time has become an invaluable source of previously unrecorded information, as well as being one of the greatest living experts on the navigation and specialized seamanship required around the coasts of Scotland. Quite a record for a lad who left school at 14 to be a message boy.

Hesperus, *commissioned in 1939 and in service with the Northern Lighthouse Board until 1963.*

THE LAST LIGHTKEEPERS

Only twice in its history has the Northern Lighthouse Board called upon someone completely outside the service to report to them on how best to select men for the particular demands of lighthouse keeping. Professor Madigan's report of 1886 dwelt, as we saw, largely on physic and physique. The second report, commissioned in 1980 from the University of Wales Ergonomics Research Unit and presented to the Board in 1984, was prompted by other concerns.

For the first hundred years, the Board's 'family' of lightkeepers, technicians and sailors grew as the technology of lights improved and more and more manned lighthouses were built. That technology can now keep more lights burning with a far smaller workforce. It is the common dilemma of the Western world in the 20th century. But how does one dismantle 'the family', or, rather, build another composed of technicians and administrators, skilled sailors and helicopter pilots, but without the men who have been the very backbone of the service since Thomas Smith appointed Keeper James Park in 1787?

In this present century of rapid change, to begin with at least, some factors of the lightkeeper's life remained relatively unaltered. It was, and often still is, a problem for the families to integrate with a community when they have to move house so regularly, uprooting themselves to move sometimes to the other end of the country, a long way from newly made friends. But perhaps it was the children of the service rather than their parents who regretted most the final departure of the families from lonely outposts such as Earraid was.

The happy boyhood memories of lightkeeper Finlay MacEachern — a surname famous in the service — accord ill with adult recollections of disputes between the Skerryvore and Dubh Artach families thrown

Mrs McDonald, the last schoolmistress on Earraid, in 1945 with her pupils, the children of the keepers at Dubh Artach and Skerryvore Lighthouses.

upon each other's isolated company. Depending upon the prevailing atmosphere, Earraid was dubbed either Harmony Row or Hell Alley! Certainly, living was primitive — no flush toilets, no hot water, no piped drinking water. One present-day keeper's wife has a vivid memory of the terrible jealousy aroused in neighbours along that lonely little street because her house had a concrete step before its door and the other homes didn't! But if mountains were made out of such molehills, deep and lifelong friendships could also grow out of the mutual dependence such remoteness imposed. Illness in any house meant a great communal rolling up of sleeves and cleaning and washing and baking and caring on behalf of the afflicted household.

For the children, though, life on Earraid had few cares. Finlay MacEachern remembers a good schooling under the remarkable Miss McKechnie in the late 1920s: 'She was a rather small frail-looking old lady, very peculiarly dressed I thought, with a very long coat, wellington boots (the weather was lovely and dry), and an enormous otter-skin hat. . . . It was with a bit of wonderment and curiosity that we entered the schoolroom in that tiny one-roomed school. . . . She took the *Glasgow Herald* to school every morning, and I had to stand at her desk and read aloud for about ten minutes each day, noting down in a notebook any word I didn't know the meaning of. So in this way I was introduced to politics, economics, foreign affairs, court proceedings etc and I did learn much more from the *Herald* than from the *Reader* that I'd had in my city school. "Did you have a gymnasium at your last school?" "Yes, Ma'am," I replied. "Thought so! Well, I don't approve of them; physical training should not be done in a stuffy room. A good walk up the hill to the lookout tower will do you a lot more good, swinging the arms from the shoulder and breathing deeply."'

The educational needs of the families were always a considerable concern for the Board. Lighthouses near schools or with shore stations near schools became known as Schooling Stations, and care is taken to send men with school-age families to these stations, although the policy of moving the men each four or five years does sometimes mean a move at a critical stage in a child's education, and often keepers have found it necessary to leave an older child behind in the care of another family until O Grades or Highers are completed.

This was not a problem in the era when the legal school-leaving age was 12. A £10 annual boarding allowance was normally paid to the fathers of children living just too far from a school. Special grants were frequently made to older children for higher education. These grants were, on occasion, made by special intercession of the Commissioners on their return from their annual voyage.

It has long been a justifiable source of pride in the service that lighthouse bairns have not suffered by their experiences of isolation and chequered education. Indeed, the evidence is distinctly to the contrary. The children of the lights have distinguished themselves down the centuries in every field of service and academic achievement. Doctors, teachers, politicians, nurses, soldiers, engineers, master mariners, explorers, scientists, and writers number in their ranks. Few graduation days in Edinburgh go by without a visit to 84 by a proud keeper and his wife and newly capped son or daughter.

Mrs Peggy Buchan, daughter of PLK Norman McLeod, reminiscing about her life as a lightkeeper's daughter, wrote that she had never been at a truly isolated station. Born on Stroma in 1929, she was a babe in arms when her father was sent to the Flannan Islands and the family moved into the Shore Station at Breasclete: 'There were four families and numerous children at the station. At that time the keepers were on the rock two months and ashore one month. Dad seemed a stranger every time he came home. Once he grew a moustache on the rock, and when he came back I refused to have anything to do with him. . . . My father liked the Flannan Isles. When he was there the keepers baked their own bread. They would also take out a live sheep and butcher it, making black puddings, mealy puddings, etc. Once when the relief was overdue and tobacco supplies had run out, the occasional keeper cut out the pocket where he usually carried his tobacco and chewed it.'

Peggy was 5 when the family moved to Scurdie Ness at Montrose. Here there were two families, and the PLK lived upstairs while the McLeods — Mr and Mrs plus Peggy and her two older brothers — lived downstairs. Here she went to school at Ferryden, a mile away. 'At Scurdie Ness the washing was done in wooden tubs and there was no running water. Usually the water was collected in a tank, from the roofs, but in a dry summer it had to be carried from a well about a quarter of a mile away. I did my bit to help by carrying a couple of milk flagons while my mother carried pails. Drinking water was brought to the lighthouse from Montrose by a Mr Scott in an old Ford lorry.

'In summer lots of holiday makers came to visit the lighthouse. Sometimes the keepers got tired of climbing that high tower and sent the older children to do the honours. We were all trained not to touch the brass rails going up and down the stairs! My mother had no head for heights and never climbed the tower.

'One drawback was that relatives were seldom near at hand. When news came of our shift from Scurdie I was inconsolable. My brothers tried to cheer me by telling me that at our next place, Tiumpan Head on Lewis, I'd be able to cry in Gaelic! It didn't help much.

'This is the first flitting I really remember. Essential furniture was provided by the NLB, but since it was pretty basic keepers always had some furniture to move, plus curtains, floor coverings, bedding, etc. Although most lighthouse houses look fairly similar, floors and windows were never exactly the same. Shortening curtains was OK — lengthening them was a different matter. Floor coverings were usually linoleum, and it wasn't unusual to have different patterns in the same room, or patched bits covered with rugs.

'Shortly after we arrived at Tiumpan, the annual stores arrived. The lighthouse itself stood on a headland near cliffs. The stores were landed at the lighthouse pier at Portnaguran, where there was also a lighthouse store. The stores were transported by a local shopkeeper who owned a rather decrepit white horse. He also owned a bus, and it was used for transporting the stores. My brother Andrew and I had a great time going back and fore in the bus. When the boxes of stores were being unpacked we were kept occupied as runners. . . .

'We went to Aird school, two miles away. Local people referred to the PLK as Captain and the ALK as the Mate, so I was the Captain's daughter. . . . The people were extremely kind, and we were made welcome in any house we visited. In summer if we went visiting or even if we went along the road to the shop we seldom came home empty-handed. People would catch us passing and give us milk, crowdie, butter, perhaps buttermilk or cream.

'At the beginning of the War, it was decided to make Tiumpan a fog signal station so there was the excitement and upheaval of building work going on. The engineer in charge of putting in the engines stayed with us. The Navy gave the keepers an Aldis lamp. It was used once to my knowledge. One fine summer morning a phone call came asking the keepers to signal to a ship which we recognized as the *Ark Royal* Try as they might they couldn't attract its attention till my brother had the bright idea of using a mirror. Having got the ship's attention, the lamp was used to pass on the message, and the ship turned back. That night Mum insisted on listening to Lord Haw-Haw, whom Dad detested. The *Ark Royal* had been sunk, yet again!

'The phone, of course, was a novelty to me. I never used it, of course, but it hung there on the wall — separate receiver and mouthpiece and a handle to turn. When the phone rang, everyone stopped what they were doing to count the rings: 1 — the exchange, 2 — Bayble Post Office, 3 — Portnaguran Post Office, 4 — Lighthouse. Later it grew more complicated when the coastguard, schoolmaster and policeman got phones.'

In 1943 the McLeods moved to Arbroath Signal Tower, the Shore Station for the Bell Rock, then in 1944 to Holburn Head and finally, in 1946, to Chanonry Point, Fortrose: 'I think Chanonry was the most beautiful station we were at. Dad sometimes set lobster creels and I'd go with him and row between the creels while he emptied them, if he was lucky, and rebaited them. He also trained me to light the lamp and put it out, and occasionally I did those things for him if he was busy.

'In 1947 I went off to University, and a year later Dad retired. It seemed strange to come home to a house in a street, and I missed the great freedom of the lighthouse life.'

Norman McLeod, Principal Lightkeeper at Chanonry Point in 1947 and father of Peggy Buchan, striking the lighthouse flag after a warship had passed.

THE WORLD WARS AND THE LIGHTS

Naturally the lights were extinguished most of the time in both wars —
but this did not mean the keepers could be off watch. The lights were
often needed to guide the exit and arrival of convoys. The lighthouses
were excellent ready-made depots — and lodgings — for Admiralty
coastguards in both wars, and the extra work of feeding more mouths
fell heavily on the PLK and ALKs' wives.

The rudimentary state of fast communications in the First World
War gave rise to at least one memorable incident. On 27 October 1915,
the cruiser *Argyll*, with 658 men on board, was sailing towards the
naval dockyard at Rosyth, and a signal was sent requesting the lighting
of the Bell Rock light. Just after 4 a.m. on the 28th, there was a mighty
crashing judder, and at dawn, the keepers, who had received no signal
to light the lamp, were horrified to find the stranded ship almost
literally on their doorstep and breaking up fast. Daring seamanship by
the crews of rescue ships and the extraordinary bravery of the keepers
in securing lines meant that not a single life was lost. The force of the
waves on that wild night was such that the *Argyll* was actually lifted
and spun right round before she finally died.

The First World War spurred the development of improved
wireless and telephone communications and, as we have seen,
revolutionized emergency communications in the lighthouse service.
And in the years after 1918 it became clear that the War had wrought
other and less obvious changes in attitudes and expectations.

It had been the practice of the NLB for some considerable time to
take on to their roster each year up to a dozen lightkeeper recruits —
called 'Expectants' if they passed muster after a three-month unpaid
training period. Once on the Expectants' list, these men simply had to
wait until an Assistant's place fell vacant, in the interim returning to
their former jobs if they could. To have undergone that three-month
training, most men would have had to abandon their previous
employment, and in the Depression years of the 1920s and 30s it
became simply unreasonable to expect a man to sacrifice paid
employment in this way. Thus it was that the NLB adopted the Trinity
House system of following the initial three-month training with a
positive offer of employment.

The Second World War was total war. Civilians as well as the armed
forces in Britain found themselves on the front line — and particularly
vulnerable were the men of the lighthouses and the lightship.
The menace became almost immediately evident when Barns Ness
Lighthouse near Dunbar was one of the first places in Britain to be the
object of enemy machine-gun attack from the air. In the spring of 1940,
when Germany had occupied Denmark and Norway, the more
northerly lights became the targets, Duncansby Head being the first of
them to be raked by airborne machine-gun fire. Twice, mines drifted
ashore at Buchan Ness, exploded and caused damage but no loss of
life. In 1941, Kinnaird Head, Stroma, Out Skerries, Auskerry, Pentland
Skerries, the Bell Rock, Corsewall, Holburn Head and Fair Isle North
and Fair Isle South all suffered bombing attacks.

It is particularly poignant that the NLB casualties were women and
children. At Fair Isle South on 21 December 1941, the wife of ALK
Sutherland was killed and her baby daughter hurt. At Out Skerries, the
mother of the Attending Boatman died three days later of wounds she
had received in the bombing there. Only six weeks later, at Fair Isle

South once again, there was an attack during which PLK Smith's wife and daughter were killed when a bomb struck the houses.

These women of the lights, who had elected to remain with their husbands and share the known dangers of the service in war, have not been forgotten. Each November, Mrs Bagg, wife of the House Officer at 84 George Street, decorates the great table at the headquarters' entrance with an arrangement of white flowers and red poppies in their memory. They have no other memorial.

There were, of course, brighter moments in the War. Peggy Buchan's father was at the Bell Rock from 1943 to 1944, and she recalls one totally unofficial event: 'Some naval vessels stationed at Arbroath occasionally called at the Bell Rock when they were on patrol, weather and tide permitting. They would give the keepers newspapers, etc., and if they knew in advance that they might be going that way, they gave the keepers' families the chance of sending out letters or perhaps a home-baked scone or other titbit.

'One very exciting Sunday they risked taking out a boatload of visitors — the wives and families of the keepers and, I think, the wife and daughter of the vessel's skipper. It was a beautiful summer's morning as we made our way in smallish groups to the harbour, embarked on the vessel and went below. The element of secrecy added to the excitement and enjoyment of the trip. Once out of the harbour we were allowed to emerge and look around.

'Landing on the iron grating, we had to watch our feet as it was so slippery. Thinking back, I can't imagine how twenty or so visitors all got into the tower at one time. We must have been in different apartments at different times.

'We were shown a special flag which had been embroidered by some womenfolk of the Stevenson family I think. It had the Bell Rock Lighthouse in the centre with two other designs on either side.'

The lightkeepers of the Bell Rock and their families in the 1950s with the Bell Rock flag, embroidered by Jane Stevenson, Robert Stevenson's wife and daughter of Thomas Smith.

In January 1947 the keepers at Dubh Artach could not be relieved because of bad weather. Two small planes were used to drop parcels of food to the marooned men.

Just up the coast from Arbroath, there had been something of an Ealing Comedy going on at the Scurdie Ness light. After several bombing raids on the area, the locals made up their minds that the keepers were in some way signalling to the enemy. There were several angry confrontations with the keepers, who tried to explain that the light was only lit, at the Navy's request, to aid convoys. Even the RAF got involved in the argument, siding with the people of Montrose and Ferryden by saying that the white lighthouse, even in daylight, was a landmark which no doubt the Germans were using. Not long after, some sailors arrived at Scurdie Ness carrying buckets of black paint and instructions to paint the tower. When they saw the rope cradle which the keepers used to do their annual lime-washing, they point-blank refused to go up and begin the job, so it was the keepers themselves, protesting, who had to paint their lovingly whitened tower black.

Not just guiding sailors on their way but rescuing them from shipwreck and drowning has been an accepted part of the keeper's life since the service began. Many keepers have received honours and awards for life-saving exploits. In wartime, the keepers looking out at every edge of Scotland were responsible for some remarkable rescues, saving the lives of many shipwrecked sailors and of airmen trying to reach shore after ditching in the sea. And in postwar years, many a weekend sailor has been grateful for the watchful men in the lighthouses seeing their difficulties and summoning help.

In the forty or so years since the end of the Second World War, the speed of change in the service has accelerated. From a simple matter like the invention of ultra-heat-treated milk to helicopter reliefs, so much has happened to render rock life, for instance, more supportable.

The usefulness of helicopters to the service was early recognized, and today almost all rock reliefs are done by this means. The hours of duty have been gradually reduced. At rock stations now there are six keepers, relieved in rotation, with one month of duty and one month's leave. Helicopter reliefs have almost made the dread R4 a thing of the past — Relief Day plus four was when a keeper knew there would be no more attempts to make a relief until the next scheduled relief day.

The policy of housing the families together in shore stations in centres of population has also been pursued as far as practicable. This has sometimes led the Board sadly to part with some of their more

The living room of Skerryvore Lighthouse with Supernumary Fred Porch, PLK Billy Rosie and Assistant Keeper John Wilson.

famous buildings, such as the Bell Rock Signal Station at Arbroath which is now a fine museum with a splendid series of exhibits on the building of the lighthouse. The signal tower at Hynish is now, too, a museum belonging to the Hebridean Trust and recording the history of the construction of Skerryvore Lighthouse.

The regular housemoving remains the *bête noire* of many a keeper's wife, but at least today the moves are made by road wherever possible and families are now rarely left awaiting stormbound tenders carrying all their goods and chattels.

The shore station improvements have been complemented to a considerable extent by attempts to make life in the lighthouses more tolerable. UHT milk and other advances in food-preservation technology have helped enormously to vary the diet on the rocks. In recent years fridges and freezers have made their appearance, helping the range of 'fresh' food available. Island sheep may now safely graze!

Many improvements have been made in sanitary arrangements, but some things, and places, cannot be changed. At the Bell Rock, the washing facilities are almost as primitive as they ever were, and keepers coming off after a four-week stint make straight for the showers on the tender and will stand under the hot water for half an hour or more!

There is a delightful, and true, tale told of a Commissioners' visit to Skerryvore in recent times, when the late Sheriff John Lillie, making his very last voyage of inspection, earnestly asked the PLK what could be done to improve life on the rock. 'A flushing toilet,' the PLK immediately replied. The good sheriff looked perplexed and thoughtful, then replied, 'I doubt, I doubt if we could manage that — what about a gas fridge instead?'

Although some aspects of the conditions of service have changed quite radically in recent years, a lightkeeper's work still has but one end, and that is the maintenance and showing of the light.

RULES AND REGULATIONS

The Northern Lighthouse Board's Service Regulations are contained in a sizeable book in which rules are laid down for every aspect of the conduct of the work, from the duties of the Principal Keeper and the various responsibilities of his staff to the setting of the station clocks. Sundials finally became redundant on the arrival of BBC time signals.

In the Routine Duties section, top priority is given to cleaning. 'The optical apparatus, lantern panes and Lightroom machinery are to be thoroughly cleaned every day, particular attention being paid to polishing the glass and bright work. . . . When cleaning in the Lightroom has been done, everything should be left in readiness for lighting.'

The cleaning duties do not, of course, end with the light. Everything from the fog signal and the radar beacon to the stairs, the engine and radio rooms, stores, doors, lawns, grounds and so on, have to be kept spick and span — with everything done by 12 noon.

Equally important is the efficiency of the light. 'Constant vigilance and attention to all the details of Lightroom duty are required of Lightkeepers in order that the light may be kept at its maximum efficiency. . . . If the lantern panes become obscured by spray, snow or any other cause they should be cleaned as soon as possible.' That cleaning can mean having to go outside the lamproom on to the tiny balcony ledge in the wildest weather.

The routine is worked out so that no man is on night watch for more than four hours at a stretch. There are specific rules on making Monthly Returns and weather reports, on flying the NLB flag, on opening the lighthouse to visitors, on how to receive Royal visitors, on ensuring provisions are ordered in time for the reliefs, and so on.

Breaches of the rules have always been severely dealt with and are very rare. A keeper who lost the mail bag — it was swept away from him in terrible weather conditions on a Flannan Isles relief in 1911 — was severely reprimanded despite having lost all his clothes as well in the accident. Even a letter of explanation from James Cadger, by then Master of the *Pole Star*, telling how the men were almost swept away with the baggage by being 'unexpectedly overwhelmed' by the sea did not prevent a salvo from Mr Peddie, the Secretary of the day: 'The Mail Bag should invariably be kept in a place of undoubted safety until taken charge of by the keeper coming ashore.' Undoubted safe places were relatively scarce on the Flannans.

Major Elliot, the American who made his Report to the Senate in 1873, noted that 'The regulations affecting the keepers of the Northern Lights are quite severe, and for any neglect of duty or other misconduct the keeper is peremptorily dismissed or otherwise punished, and a printed circular, advising keepers of the facts in the case is at once sent to all the stations in the service. The warning thus received tends greatly to promote the efficiency and good management of the lights.' A man can still be dismissed for falling asleep on lightroom watch.

LEISURE TIME

The University of Wales Ergonomic Research Unit Report of 1984 noted the hobbies and interests of modern lightkeepers. Nobody appears to indulge in the old lighthouse craft of putting ships in bottles, and some of the ploys, such as CB radio and watching television, are strictly 20th century, but down the years some hobbies have remained constant: wood-turning, lamp-making, stamp-collecting, fly-tying, painting in oils, watercolours or pen and ink, bird-watching, ship-watching, and chess. Photography, reading and

Norrie Muir, Principal Lightkeeper at the Isle of May, pulling the blinds round the light at sunrise.

gardening come very high on the list. The Board, with the help of the libraries service, have solved the sending of books to the stations.

Several NLB keepers have national reputations as ornithologists. Where better to observe birds of passage than on remote rocks that are often the first possible landing places for birds crossing oceans on migrations. In recent times, it has been the keepers before anyone else who have been the first to spot oil slicks and see the damage done to wildlife. Many lighthouses are now in Nature Conservancy areas, and the keepers are keen observers of the activities of seals, otter and deer.

At some rock stations sea fishing is a popular pastime, but there is one hobby not many would associate with lightkeeping, and that is golf. Several stations have their own courses of a sort. In the past, on the Isle of May there was a three-hole course, with terrible confusion caused by the thousands of puffin burrows that riddle the island. The Calf of Man course has four holes, likewise Fair Isle.

Of necessity, the keepers are weather observers — a duty that began almost with the service. The official link with meteorological study began when the Board agreed to provide information to the Scottish Meteorological Society when it was founded in 1857. The tradition of recording rainfall information for the British Rainfall Organisation began in 1862 and continued until that was taken over in 1919 by the Meteorological Office, now a Government department in the Ministry of Defence. The Met Office also took over the Scottish Meteorological Society's work in 1920 and found the lighthouses were providing a stream of weather information unrivalled in the world.

Today, several light stations round our coasts provide the Met Office with real-time data, and the Bell Rock has a full wind-recording device and is one of the stations making hourly weather reports. The Meteorological Office, whose work is now much changed by satellite information, computer analysed, still rely very largely on these coastal reports, particularly for local weather. Cloud cover in these northern realms can make satellite readings relatively unreliable on occasions.

This service is backed up by the monthly weather reports every station must send in to 84 George Street along with the Monthly Returns. The observations of weather conditions are invaluable records for use not only by meteorologists but by the legal profession dealing with cases where the prevailing weather on a particular day may be a vital factor. No matter how sophisticated automatic weather recording may become in future years, the Met Office do not view the progressive demanning of the lights with equanimity.

For two hundred years, the men in the lighthouses have not only watched and noted the weather, they have quite voluntarily provided extra pairs of eyes surveying the coast and the movements of shipping, and alerting lifeboat and coastguard help for ships and people in distress. It is with some perplexity that these other services view the future when there will still be bright and shining lights for the safety of all, but the watchful eyes will have gone.

No career keepers have been recruited since 1981, and it has been agreed between the men's representatives and the Board that there will be no redundancies and that the lightkeeper service will be reduced by natural wastage. It is highly probable that not many years from now lighthouse keeping will have passed into history and into folklore, too, for the men who abided by their motto, *In Salutem Omnium*, 'For the Safety of All', and kept the lights burning bright became amongst the most respected men in the Scottish community.

TWO HUNDRED YEARS ON

The Pharos *in evening dress for the Commissioners' Inspection Tour.*

As the Commissioners sailed into their second century, that miserable summer of 1886, they probably had few doubts in their minds that the great service which they led was on course for a second century of business as usual. And to a certain extent they would have been correct in that assumption. The service has continued to build lights — sometimes after lengthy wrangles with Trinity House and the Board, later Department, of Trade. It has continued never to lose sight of the aims and objectives of its function. But what those good provosts and sheriffs could not have foreseen was how social and technological revolutions plus two world wars in the 20th century would affect the work of the Northern Lighthouse Board. As they sailed the northern seas that dank summer, they could never have imagined the waters dotted with oil platforms nor oil tanker routes marked by their lights and beacons and buoys. They might have been amused to think of Hynish or the Arbroath Signal Stations as museums, but pained at the thought that when the old lights are automated so much fine woodwork, dearly paid for, has to be pulled out as a fire precaution.

Trade depressions, slumps, changes in trading patterns have all affected the operation and the finances of the Northern Lighthouse Board — although the early Commissioners were no strangers to financial difficulty. With the passing of the Merchant Shipping Act of 1898, however, the Commissioners must have had great satisfaction in the knowledge that from then on the collected dues would once again revert to being used exclusively for lighthouse purposes.

Some years later, a Royal Commission on Lighthouse Administration was set up, after which Trinity House was obliged to consider proposals put to them by the Commissioners of Northern Lighthouses mainly from a nautical point of view. This effectively helped to smooth the NLB's ruffled feathers over what they had seen as Trinity House overbearance in Scottish and Manx building and planning matters. A Lights Advisory Committee was also set up, formed of representatives of chambers of commerce and shipping interests. Today, it is only after formal consultation with those who use and need Scottish lighthouses — shipping companies, fishermen, yachtsmen, the Royal Navy, the lifeboat and coastguard services — that any proposal for new lights is put forward to Trinity House and the Department of Trade.

The changing needs of the service have led to considerable changes in that administration and organization. The original administrative headquarters at 84 George Street remain but in the 1970s were extensively enlarged and altered behind the handsome Georgian facade. Today, the douce, Edinburgh New Town frontage with its elegant windows and glorious summer window boxes, with its flags of the United Kingdom, Scotland and the Isle of Man, and its working model of a pillar lighthouse twinkling above the door, conceals not only fine offices but a large electrical and electronic workshop, drawing and design departments. Here, right in the heart of one of the most historic streets in Europe is, quite unsuspected by the passer-by, a hive of industry building and testing new lighthouse equipment.

84 George Street, Edinburgh, headquarters of the Northern Lighthouse Board.

Beginning in 1786 with Thomas Smith, ten men have been Engineer to the Board. In 1972 the title was changed to Engineer-in-Chief. For some years the Secretary to the Board also had the title General Manager. Since 1964 the two posts have been separate. Until 1961, the Secretary/General Managers were almost all lawyers — Writers to the Signet or advocates. In 1961, a retired Royal Navy Lieutenant Commander, W. Alastair Robertson CBE, DSC, was appointed, and he was succeeded in 1977 by the present General Manager, another retired Royal Navy man, Commander John M. Mackay MBE. Commander Mackay is only the ninth man to hold this office since John Gray was appointed at that first meeting of the Trustees in August 1786. The Board's first Welfare Officer, Eric Omand, was appointed in 1972. He had been a lightkeeper for twenty-eight years and was one of the last to leave Earraid when it was given up in 1952.

The composition of the Commissioners has also altered in response to the times. Local government and sheriffdom reorganization in the 1970s and the necessity to have members of the Board with some comprehension of the new technologies that were becoming so important to its work prompted these changes. In 1974, an Act of Parliament added, for the very first time, a representative from the Isle of Man, and allowed the Board to elect four, and later five, additional members to the new list of Commissioners, somewhat depleted by the abolition of Bailies under the Local Government (Scotland) Act of 1973. The sheriffdoms, too, had been reduced, from twelve to six, and although the Lord Provosts of Edinburgh, Aberdeen and Glasgow remained, old offices, such as Provost of Inverness and Provost of Campbeltown, which had been on the 1786 list, had vanished, their places taken in the end by appropriate district council representatives.

Each July the Commissioners still make a voyage round their domain, not all of it in one short cruise, but usually about a third of

The Commissioners entering their third century.

the lights are visited by them annually. The object of these visits will obviously change as the lights are demanned, but in the meantime their chief concern is still the men and their families and the conditions of the lights. Peggy Buchan remembers: 'There was always some tension in the air when the annual inspection was due. Officially they were not announced beforehand, but the bush telegraph was quite efficient! Everything had to be spick and span so we were dared to disarrange anything. If a visit was expected we were hauled out of bed at an early hour. Meals might be early or late. The grown-ups really dreaded the inspections. On the other hand, the children looked forward to the Commissioners' visits because they always brought sweets with them for us.'

In the summer of 1986, as in almost every other July for two hundred years, the Commissioners of Northern Lighthouses will set sail in their commodore ship. On 1 August, somewhere at Scotland's edge, they sail into their third century, their realm on that day comprising 39 manned stations, 45 major automatic lights and 102 minor automatic lights. Future passages may be stormy, for total automation represents some uncharted waters with hidden reefs, but behind them lie two hundred years of extraordinary achievement.

For the safety of all they built some of the most remarkable structures ever engineered. For the safety of all was created a service demanding, and getting, self-sacrifice, courage and total devotion to duty on the part of its staff. For the safety of all, in peace and in war, the kindly Northern Lights have swept a bright path for the men of the sea.

PHOTOGRAPHS AND TEXT
by
KEITH ALLARDYCE

My journey around some of the lighthouses at
Scotland's edge began by chance, in Orkney, in
1974. I came to stay on Copinsay, in the island's
long-deserted farmhouse where my only
neighbours were the keepers of Copinsay
Lighthouse. I discovered there, and beyond, a
special way of life which I hope I have captured
here.

Keith Allardyce

FLANNAN ISLANDS

The Flannan Islands, fifteen miles west of the Outer Hebrides, are some of Scotland's loneliest rocks. Also known as the Seven Hunters, their dark ghostly shapes lie desolate and mysterious. On Eilean Mor, the largest, stands the lighthouse. Every half-minute, every night, its light gives two flashes out into the Atlantic gloom.

There have been no lightkeepers on the Flannans since 1971. The last three keepers to spend their duty at the lighthouse were taken off the rock by helicopter that year, after automatic machinery had been installed by the engineers of the Lighthouse Board.

In December 1900, one year after the light had been lit for the first time, the three keepers of the Flannans disappeared. The Lighthouse Vessel *Hesperus* was at the rock for a routine visit on 26 December before the tragedy was discovered.

No sign of life could be seen when the ship arrived. Assistant Keeper Joseph Moore, the relieving keeper at the time, was sent ashore to investigate. The superintendent's report tells us, 'When he went up to the station, he found the entrance gate and the outside doors closed, the clock stopped, no fire lit, and, looking into the bedrooms, he found the beds empty'. Moore ran back to the landing to tell the crew of the *Hesperus*. With two of them, he returned to the lighthouse for a more thorough search.

It was established that the routine of the station had carried on normally until 15 December: 'The last entry on the slate had been made by Mr Ducat, the Principal Keeper, on the morning of Saturday 15 December. The lamp was trimmed, the oil fountains and canteens filled up, and the lens machinery cleaned.'

Many explanations have been given for the disappearance — some practical, others romantic. The most probable is that all three keepers had been working at the landing, or on the crane platform, when a huge wave which had built up in the gulley exploded across them and swept them into the sea. Many keepers since the tragedy have experienced this wave phenomenon. Bert Petrie, now Principal Keeper at Duncansby Head Lighthouse, tells of how he and the other two keepers were painting the crane and railings in the Flannans landing gulley, over one hundred feet above sea level, when a wave suddenly swept over them. Two of them were knocked off their feet but managed to hold on to the railings, while the third scrambled higher up the rock side.

There can be no conclusive evidence of what happened to the three keepers in 1900; their disappearance will remain a mystery, but Joseph Moore's search of the lighthouse with his two companions from the *Hesperus* has become known throughout the world in W. W. Gibson's poem, which ends:

> 'We seemed to stand for an endless while,
> Though still no word was said,
> Three men alive on Flannan Isle
> Who thought on three men dead'.

ESTABLISHED:	▶ *1899*
TYPE:	▶ *Major automatic (1971)*
ENGINEER:	▶ *D. Alan Stevenson*
POSITION:	▶ *58° 17.3' N 7° 35.4' W, on Eilean Mor island, one of a group of seven, 15 miles northwest of Lewis.*
CHARACTER:	▶ *Flashing 2 white every 30 seconds*
ELEVATION:	▶ *101 metres*
NOMINAL RANGE:	▶ *20 miles*
STRUCTURE:	▶ *White tower, 23 metres high*

EILEAN GLAS

'That first winter was terrible,' said Mary Fraser. Len, her husband, had just been appointed keeper at Eilean Glas. They were landed on the island of Scalpay, in June 1972 and were to live there for five years, sharing this remote corner of the island, off the east coast of Harris in the Outer Hebrides, with two other lighthouse families. 'Between Christmas and the New Year saw the worst storms. On 29 December, the waves started crashing over the courtyard walls.'

'I was in the engine room changing watch,' said Len. 'It was 6 a.m.' His wife was alone in the house. 'Water suddenly started pouring in through the windows and under the door,' Mary recalled. 'I opened the door to fetch Len, but a huge wave hit me as I stepped outside. I ran into the kitchen and just sat down and cried.' Later that day, the local assistant keeper phoned Len to say that he was unable to cross the moor from the village to go on watch. The storm had by now reached force twelve. Len covered his colleague's watch for him later that night — 10 p.m. to 2 a.m.

'We were happy at Scalpay, though. They were the happiest years of our lives. We had a good crew — that's what made it so wonderful. We all got on well, and we had to help each other. We were never lonely there. Once a month we'd go to Stornoway. First we had to walk over the moor to meet the taxi on the road. If we had been soaked on the moor, then someone in the village would take our coats and dry them for us until we came back. Sometimes we would stay with our friends at the halfway house if the weather was too bad to cross the moor back to the lighthouse.

'The grocer came to the lighthouse once a week in his boat. If he couldn't make it by boat, then he and another man would carry the groceries on their backs and walk instead. Once a week we'd go to the village to collect the meat.

'Our first summer saw the arrival of the Lighthouse Commissioners on the *Pharos,* on their annual cruise of inspection. Our son started his first job on that ship. When the *Pharos* sailed, he sailed with them. Then our daughter left us when she left Stornoway school the following year. We were back to square one again then, just the two of us.'

ESTABLISHED:	▶ 1789
TYPE:	▶ Major automatic (1978)
ENGINEER:	▶ Thomas Smith
POSITION:	▶ 57° 51.4' N 6° 38.5' W, on the island of Scalpay in the Outer Hebrides
CHARACTER:	▶ Flashing 3 white every 20 seconds
ELEVATION:	▶ 43 metres
NOMINAL RANGE:	▶ 23 miles
STRUCTURE:	▶ White tower, 30 metres high with red bands
FOGHORN:	▶ Blast of 4.5 seconds every 45 seconds

STOER HEAD

Now an automatic lighthouse, until 1976 Stoer Head was a family station, but it was remote and, being a two-man station, lonely. John Boath, today a Principal at the Bell Rock, was an Assistant Keeper here and recalls the birth of one of his children at the lighthouse. 'I was all prepared to deliver the baby myself, it was back in December 1969. The weather was really bad. But the midwife and doctor arrived just in time.'

Audrey Lord, who lives about a mile from the lighthouse, is now the Attendant Keeper, and she visits it once a week to check the apparatus in the tower. She and Mrs Martin, Attendant Keeper at Ardtreck, a minor lighthouse across the Minch on Skye, are the only two women keepers in the service. The lightkeepers' houses at Stoer Head are now holiday homes for staff of the Northern Lighthouse Board, and they are also offered to the staff of Trinity House and the Commissioners of Irish Lights.

'It was one of the old-style lights,' says John Clark, the Administration Officer of the Northern Lighthouse Board. 'It was a family station, but was so remote it was never a popular place with the keepers or their families. It's a great place for a holiday, though. I've been there several times with my family.'

There are two separate houses by the tower, and John Clark has met others holidaying there, including a keeper, a radio technician, and a ship's greaser. 'It's so quiet, so away from it all,' says John. 'As the sun sets and the sky darkens, you can see from the front room the lighthouse beams sweeping across the sea.'

79

ESTABLISHED:	▶ *1870*
TYPE:	▶ *Major automatic (1978)*
ENGINEER:	▶ *David and Thomas Stevenson*
POSITION:	▶ *58° 14.4′ N 5° 24′ W*
CHARACTER:	▶ *Flashing white every 15 seconds*
ELEVATION:	▶ *59 metres*
NOMINAL RANGE:	▶ *24 miles*
STRUCTURE:	▶ *White tower, 14 metres high*

NEIST POINT

On the westernmost headland of the Isle of Skye stands Neist Point Lighthouse. A long narrow road winds over moorland and bog towards it but stops abruptly at the top of a high crag. From there a footpath cuts below the crag and round a huge outcrop of rock to reach the lighthouse at the edge of a cliff. The lighthouse was changed from a family station to a six-man 'rock-relieving' station in 1975. It is run like a rock station yet is easily accessible at any time.

Murdoch Lamont is a Principal Keeper at Neist Point. He has two brothers who are also Principal Keepers in the service. 'During my last time here, from 1963 to 1968 as an Assistant Lightkeeper, I got married and our son was born. This was my family's home ' said Murdoch, indicating the quarters which he now shares with two other keepers. His son has now grown up and is serving in the RAF, but his wife lives at the Shore Station in Portree, on the other side of Skye.

The foghorn blasted in the morning light. It was the weekly Monday foghorn practice. Its eerie bellows echoed between the rocks around Neist and over Moonen Bay. Three whooper swans, wild swans from the north, flew overhead and added their mournful cries to the autumn wind.

Principal Keeper Murdoch Lamont, left, and Assistant Keepers Rab Kyle and Billy Baillie. The dog, Struan, is named after the village between Neist and Portree.

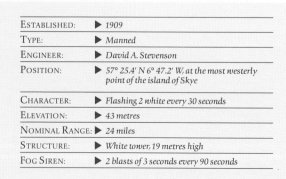

ESTABLISHED:	▶ 1909
TYPE:	▶ Manned
ENGINEER:	▶ David A. Stevenson
POSITION:	▶ 57° 25.4' N 6° 47.2' W, at the most westerly point of the island of Skye
CHARACTER:	▶ Flashing 2 white every 30 seconds
ELEVATION:	▶ 43 metres
NOMINAL RANGE:	▶ 24 miles
STRUCTURE:	▶ White tower, 19 metres high
FOG SIREN:	▶ 2 blasts of 3 seconds every 90 seconds

ORNSAY

Donald Edwards was Attendant Keeper for Ornsay until he retired at the end of April 1986. 'Old age catches up with all of us,' he said. He would visit the light about once a week, more often when the gas cylinder fuelling the light was getting low, to try to get the most out of the cylinder in use before switching over to the next. He was given twelve cylinders a year, delivered by the *Pharos* during her annual west coast storing run. Twelve would usually last the time, except for 1985 when he needed an extra four cylinders because it was such a dark year. 'The automatic switch was switched on more often than usual. It even switches on during daylight if it happens to be a particularly dark day. It is easy enough to get in extra cylinders or any other supplies for the tower as the *Fingal* is never far away. The *Fingal* drops anything needed in a hurry.'

Donald Edwards lives nearby and it was just a short walk across to the small tidal island at low tide to check the lighthouse. The new Attendant Keeper, Richard Fowler, lives even closer, in the two lightkeepers' houses on the island, converted into one.

ESTABLISHED:	▶ *1857*
TYPE:	▶ *Minor automatic (1962)*
ENGINEER:	▶ *David and Thomas Stevenson*
POSITION:	▶ *57° 8.6' N 5° 46.4' W*
CHARACTER:	▶ *Flashing 2 white every 7 seconds*
NOMINAL RANGE:	▶ *12 miles*
STRUCTURE:	▶ *White tower, 19 metres high*

SANDAIG

Camusfearna is the name Gavin Maxwell gave to Sandaig. It is Gaelic for 'Bay of the Alders', and it was here, in a house near the shore, that Maxwell wrote his touching autobiography, *Ring of Bright Water*. At Sandaig, out beyond the shore where a burn runs into the sea a chain of small islands reaches into the Sound of Sleat. On the largest of these islands stands Sandaig Lighthouse, a minor automatic light. Opposite the islands to the west is Skye, to the south the entrance to the spectacular but foreboding Loch Hourn, and far out beyond the Sound the islands of Eigg and Rhum.

The magic of Sandaig in autumn is described in *Ring of Bright Water:* 'When the full moon comes at this season I have sat on the hillside at night and listened to the stags answering one another from hill to hill all round the horizon, a horizon of steel-grey peaks among moving silver clouds and the sea gleaming white at their feet, and high under the stars, the drifting chorus of the wild geese flying southward out of the night and the north.'

The impact that *Ring of Bright Water* had on its readers was profound. Maxwell's Sandaig was a place most people can only dream about, and he received many poignant letters following the book's publication. 'Whatever you are going to do,' read one, 'please never say that the *Camusfearna* of *Ring of Bright Water* never was. Say that it's gone, if you like, but not that you lied. I couldn't take that, because it is the only evidence I have that Paradise existed somewhere.'

Maxwell's cottage had been deserted for many years before he lived there. Originally it was occupied by a shepherd who tended Sandaig Lighthouse. He would usually walk over to the light at low tide, when the sand bars, which connect the islands to each other and to the shore, were uncovered. The cottage at Sandaig has now been destroyed. In 1969 it was gutted by fire, and later, on the eve of Maxwell's death, it was bulldozed to the ground.

A Glenelg man, Ian Campbell, travels down the Sound in his dinghy about once a fortnight to tend Sandaig Lighthouse. It is late October, and after days of storms and rain suddenly the wind has dropped and the sky has cleared. Ian Campbell's outboard engine seems to shatter the silence of the Sound. The boat is spreading a fan pattern of a wake across a glass-smooth sea. Less than a mile from Sandaig Ian notices something. 'Do you see the otters?' Two otters, a mother and a cub, are playing in the water near the shore, and they ignore us as we glide past. We climb the lighthouse ladder. From the lantern it is just possible to glimpse over the island tops into a world of rock and sea that had once been *Camusfearna*.

ESTABLISHED:	▶ 1950
TYPE:	▶ Built as a minor automatic light
POSITION:	▶ 57° 10.1' N 5° 42.2' W, at northwest point of a small island north of the mouth of Loch Hourn
CHARACTER:	▶ Flashing white every 6 seconds
ELEVATION:	▶ 12 metres
NOMINAL RANGE:	▶ 8 miles
STRUCTURE:	▶ White 8-sided tower, 7 metres high

ARDNAMURCHAN

Assistant Keepers Richard Simons, above, and Steven Granger in the lantern.

'God was short of earth when he made Ardnamurchan,' tells the poet Alasdair Maclean, 'A long peninsula of solid rock, upholstered every year in threadbare green.'

The road to the lighthouse seems to twist and turn and rise and drop for ever as it follows, more or less, the shores of Loch Sunart. Then, suddenly, around a great shoulder of rock, the road tapers into two gentle bends bounded by high walls and ends at the lighthouse.

This is the end of the peninsula, the most westerly point of the Scottish mainland. The pink tower of the lighthouse is made of granite, not the cold grey Ardnamurchan granite but a warm stone from the island of Earraid in the Ross of Mull. The stone has not been painted white in the traditional style here but has been left exposed.

In a little village craftshop a few miles from the lighthouse are all kinds of goods for sale, from earrings to health food. Stacked in a corner are some walking sticks with carved crooks, made by a local assistant keeper to the lighthouse, Ian Ramon. There is also a pile of colourful children's vests, knitted by the wife of one of the assistant keepers, and some miniature rocking chairs made from wooden clothespegs by another keeper's wife.

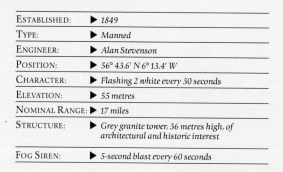

ESTABLISHED:	▶ 1849
TYPE:	▶ Manned
ENGINEER:	▶ Alan Stevenson
POSITION:	▶ 56° 43.6' N 6° 13.4' W
CHARACTER:	▶ Flashing 2 white every 30 seconds
ELEVATION:	▶ 55 metres
NOMINAL RANGE:	▶ 17 miles
STRUCTURE:	▶ Grey granite tower, 36 metres high, of architectural and historic interest
FOG SIREN:	▶ 5-second blast every 60 seconds

SKERRYVORE

'It takes about three days to unwind after I get home from here,' says Billy Rosie, Principal Keeper of Skerryvore Lighthouse. He has been stationed there for three years, doing his four weeks on and four weeks off. 'You can't walk north, south, east or west, just up and down. But we have an exercise bicycle which we all use.'

Skerryvore Lighthouse is 25 miles west of Mull, standing on a long reef which at high tide is completely covered by water. The nearest land is Tiree, about fourteen miles to the north.

Billy Rosie usually travels to the rock with Bill Gault. 'He's good company. Good for a discussion, and good for an argument. We can talk about all sorts of subjects and argue and still get on well. Being out here made one keeper feel very depressed. He was just a beginner, new to the service. He spent most of his two weeks here curled up on the kitchen windowsill, staring out to sea. Another man, an engineer, was so frightened by the noise of the wind and the sea he was afraid to go to his bunk at night. The wind rose to force nine or ten after he arrived, and you can hardly hear yourself speak in the tower then. The wind shrieks past the windows.'

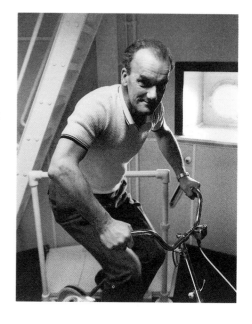

The present lens and winding machinery were put in the tower in 1959 after a fire had completely gutted the lighthouse in 1954. The keepers who were on duty at the time got out safely and were rescued from off the rocks — fortunately for them, the tide was out at the time. The heat of the fire was so strong that it even cracked the tower structure.

The new winding machinery is automatic, so once the light is switched on each evening it looks after itself although it must be checked regularly throughout the night in case anything has gone wrong. The machinery did fail recently. A governor became faulty, and the three keepers had to work one-hour shifts for two nights, pushing the lens around by hand.

Near the base of the tower and uncovered at low tide is the helicopter pad. On relief day it takes only two or three minutes for the changeover. Four weeks ashore is a pleasant prospect for the keepers at the end of their duty. Those just arriving get on with the job and start counting the days.

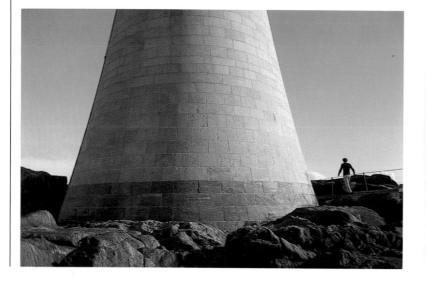

ESTABLISHED:	▶ 1844
TYPE:	▶ Manned
ENGINEER:	▶ Alan Stevenson
POSITION:	▶ 56° 19.4' N 7° 6.9' W, on small island 10 miles southwest of Tiree
CHARACTER:	▶ Flashing white every 10 seconds
ELEVATION:	▶ 46 metres
NOMINAL RANGE:	▶ 26 miles
STRUCTURE:	▶ Grey granite tower, 48 metres high
FOGHORN:	▶ 1 blast every 60 seconds

DUBH ARTACH

Jack Clark was keeper at Dubh Artach in his early years. '"The black rock" it was called, and a place most people dreaded.' Landings by the relief boat were often hazardous because of the weather, and long delays were common.

Were hobbies a kind of escape out there? 'Hobbies on the rock?' asks Jack. 'Well, reading, of course, and listening to the radio. We couldn't have the radio on all the time, though, because of the batteries. We would listen to the news, Any Questions, Round the Horne, and every Friday night there was Scottish dance music. No one missed the MacFlannels, a Scottish comedy programme in the 1950s, and Down at the Mains.'

Dubh Artach was automated in 1971, to no one's regret, and the tower is empty now of all the furnishings which once made the place a home for three people. Instead, the upper rooms are filled with large gas cylinders and banks of heavy-duty batteries. Once a year the *Fingal,* one of the lighthouse tenders, visits the rock. It lies a few hundred yards off, and a helicopter ferries men and materials from the ship to the tower to replenish the gas and the batteries and to check the automatic apparatus, using a variety of containers, including a basket for small odds and ends.

Thirty-three gas cylinders are delivered and connected into the fuelling system for the light by Wilbur MacDonald and a colleague. At the top of the granite tower, John Pirie, electrical technician, climbs the dome to check the automatic foghorn apparatus while over one hundred feet below empty gas cylinders are neatly stacked on the helicopter pad, waiting to be ferried back on board *Fingal.* The pad is on the site of the barracks lived in by the men who erected the tower during five brief building seasons before the light was lit in 1872. In the middle of the one day of activity on the now otherwise year-long deserted rock, two of the crewmen on the *Fingal* wear their firefighting suits, standard equipment in the service.

'That's how I saw Dubh Artach the last time I was out here,' said Captain Forth of the *Fingal* as he showed me the photographs he'd taken of the lighthouse from the ship that time. 'Gloomy', he said, 'Gloomy and dark. It seems to suit the place during a great storm, with rain and dark clouds all around.'

ESTABLISHED:	▶ 1872
TYPE:	▶ Major automatic (1971)
ENGINEER:	▶ Thomas and David Stevenson
POSITION:	▶ 56° 8' N 6° 37.9' W, on rock at the end of the Torran Rocks reef
CHARACTER:	▶ Flashing 2 white every 30 seconds
ELEVATION:	▶ 44 metres
NOMINAL RANGE:	▶ 20 miles
STRUCTURE:	▶ Grey granite tower, 38 metres high, with a broad red band
FOGHORN:	▶ 2 blasts every 45 seconds

FLADDA

'My father, my grandfather, my grandfather's cousin, they were all Attending Boatmen in their turn to Fladda,' says Lachlan McLachlan. They were fishermen, like Lachie, and lived on the island of Luing. Since the light was automated in 1956 he has been Attendant Keeper, taking over from his father.

Lachie's cottage at Cullipool has some of the hallmarks of being connected with the lighthouse service. His garden has the typically large and ornate clothesline posts taken from the Fladda garden after the automation; and the cottage itself and the garden wall are painted white. There is the paraphernalia of a fisherman, too, with a bush aflame with rubber gloves, bright red and orange; and lobster pots and fish boxes are scattered here and there.

It is from fishing for lobster and prawns that Lachlan McLachlan earns a living, with his boat *The Wild Rose*. He is keen to start dredging for scallops but would need a heavier boat for the work. 'It will be difficult to part with *The Wild Rose*,' says Lachie. 'Another boat might be better for the job, but it would not be so beautiful.' Once a week, Lachie lands at Fladda to check the light, the lens and the gas. He sometimes takes the youngest of his five children, Alasdair, to help with the landings, especially during the long school summer holidays. He also keeps an eye on the minor lights around the fishing grounds. There is a light on the Garvellachs, 'The Isles of the Sea', a great line of jagged rocks out to the west, and there are other lights among the skerries with beautiful Gaelic names, such as *Dubh Sgeir*, *Ruadh Sgeir* and *Reisa an t'Sruith*.

Eoghan McLachlan, Lachie's eldest son, used to accompany his father fishing, but now has his own boat. 'He'll probably follow me as Attendant Keeper at Fladda,' says Lachlan, 'but not for a while yet!'

ESTABLISHED:	▶ 1860
TYPE:	▶ Minor automatic (1956)
ENGINEER:	▶ David and Thomas Stevenson
POSITION:	▶ 56° 14.9′ N 5° 40.8′ W, on small island off the west coast of the island of Luing
CHARACTER:	▶ Flashing white every 6 seconds
ELEVATION:	▶ 13 metres
NOMINAL RANGE:	▶ White 14 miles, red 11 miles
STRUCTURE:	▶ White tower, 13 metres high

MULL OF KINTYRE

Twelve miles of dazzling steel-grey light danced above the sea between the lighthouse and the faint misty headland of Ireland to the west. Wild hairpin bends descend a thousand feet from a high pass, the Gap, to the lighthouse, clinging to the cliffside 300 feet above sea level. A notice at the lighthouse gate reads 'Lighthouse closed today'. In the lighthouse garden, carved out of the clifftop slope and only made safe by a high wall which makes you feel insecure just to look at it, a line of colourful washing is flapping wildly in the gale. Tucked in a corner of the lighthouse courtyard is the last of the white milestones which punctuate the road over the moors and down the hillside: 'Campbeltown 16 miles 1030 yds'.

Magnus Leask, a Shetlander from Yell, is the Principal Keeper here and has two assistants. This is a shore station although it is extremely remote. Once a week there is a Land-Rover run to Campbeltown for the shopping, though in winter the ascent to the Gap is often impassable with ice and snow and can close the keepers and their families in for weeks at a time.

As evening falls, the lights of Northern Ireland appear across the North Channel — Rathlin Island's east light and others a little to the south on the Antrim coast.

ESTABLISHED:	▶ 1788
TYPE:	▶ Manned
ENGINEER:	▶ Thomas Smith
POSITION:	▶ 55° 18.6' N 5° 48.1' W, at the southern tip of the Mull of Kintyre
CHARACTER:	▶ Flashing 2 white every 20 seconds
ELEVATION:	▶ 91 metres
NOMINAL RANGE:	▶ 29 miles
STRUCTURE:	▶ Yellow tower on white building, 12 metres high
FOGHORN:	▶ 2 blasts every 90 seconds

Magnus Leask, Principal Keeper.

AILSA CRAIG

'This is number twelve for me and my last,' said Billy Frazer, also known as Paddy — he is Irish — and a Principal Lighthouse Keeper for over fifteen years, not long before he retired to Ballantrae. 'In a few months I'll be living out my retirement on the Ayrshire coast opposite here, and with some luck with a view of the sea. Without the sea I don't think I could exist. I'll find it difficult at first without a lighthouse. Even now I find it difficult to sleep when I'm ashore. Out here you're in and out of your bed all hours. You're never in the same routine each day.

'I've been to some bad rocks, like Dubh Artach, the one that all keepers dreaded going to. In the early days I was stationed at the Mull of Galloway, where I met my wife. After a few shifts all around Scotland over the years, we returned there. My wife became ill and we were given the shift to Galloway, her native land, and it's there that she died. I loved the place; we both did. You can view, let me see, five kingdoms. You can see Scotland, Ireland, England, Man, and the Kingdom of Heaven. Now that's the place.

'Life was lonely then, although I moved to Fair Isle North. You were part of the community there, and you had your fellow keepers and their families at the light, but I was on my own, and then it was to Ailsa Craig, the monarch of all the lights.'

ESTABLISHED:	▶ 1886
TYPE:	▶ Manned
ENGINEER:	▶ Thomas and D. Alan Stevenson
POSITION:	▶ 55° 15.1' N 5° 6.4' W
CHARACTER:	▶ Flashing 6 white every 30 seconds
NOMINAL RANGE:	▶ 17 miles
STRUCTURE:	▶ White tower, 11 metres high, of architectural and historic interest
FOGHORN:	▶ 3 blast of 3 seconds every 45 seconds

KILLANTRINGAN

'I could have stayed there at Killantringan,' said Duncan Jordan, now Principal Lighthouse Keeper at St Abb's Head. 'Oh, it was a lovely station, a lovely station to keep clean. The local assistant used to come for his watch, and after he'd been you'd never have any brass to clean anywhere. The only time I'd polish anything was just before he came back from his holidays! Oh Christ, he kept it looking beautiful.'

The routine of the Killantringan lightkeepers was suddenly disrupted during a storm early in 1982, when the container ship *Craigantlet,* ran aground below the lighthouse at 3.45 a.m. on Friday 26 February. The crew was taken off the ship by helicopter, but there

Portpatrick, Wigtownshire, the nearest village to Killantringan.

was concern about the cargo, thought to contain dangerous chemicals. The coastguard and police kept a twenty-four hour a day watch on the wreck, and rumours about the cargo were rife around Killantringan.

Most of the cargo, held in large tanks, was washed ashore within a few days as the storm worsened. Scientists, wearing breathing apparatus, inspected the contents. It was discovered that some tanks, recorded as empty, were found to contain chemicals, and others contained chemicals which did not correspond to the cargo records.

By the fifth day of the wreck, the storm had become even worse, and some of the containers were damaged by the sea and began to leak. The next day, the emergency light was established at the lighthouse, and the lightkeepers and their wives and families were evacuated to a Stranraer hotel. It was to be forty-two days before conditions were safe for the lightkeepers to occupy the lighthouse again.

ESTABLISHED:	▶ *1900*
TYPE:	▶ *Manned*
ENGINEER:	▶ *David A. Stevenson*
POSITION:	▶ *54° 51.7′ N 5° 8.7′ W*
CHARACTER:	▶ *Flashing 2 white every 15 seconds*
NOMINAL RANGE:	▶ *25 miles*
STRUCTURE:	▶ *White tower, 22 metres high*
FOG SIREN:	▶ *3 blasts every 90 seconds*

MULL OF GALLOWAY

Second Assistant Peter Hill with his wife, Margaret, and children.

It is 8.45 a.m. on a Monday morning. School is five miles away at Drummore, and three children are waiting at the lighthouse gate for their taxi. It is bitterly cold, and a dense fog is blowing in off the sea from the west. Every minute the foghorn blasts two deep booms.

'It sounds like a coo with a sair stomach, do'ent it?' says 7-year-old Karen. 'It doesn't keep us awake at night, ye ken; we're used to it.'

First Assistant Ron Ireland is married and has a family of four children at the station. His grandfather and father were keepers, and his father-in-law is Steward on the *Fingal*. 'The character of a lighthouse is according to its light and its foghorn,' he says, 'but it also has another character, the people in it. It's always the people that make a place. There are fourteen of us here. We all get along fine.'

'I think the kids feel a bit isolated out here, but I like it myself because it's a quiet place — apart from the foghorn!' says Margaret Hill, the Second Assistant's wife. 'Sometimes the tourists ask if we have paraffin lamps in the houses. They think we live very old fashioned for some reason.'

'We have visitors that ask us, "What on earth do you do all day?" You look around and whatever you see done, we do it,' says the Principal. 'I won't say there's never a dull moment, but nearly. We get visitors from all over the world out here in the summer. Not only from Europe, but from faraway places like Borneo, Taiwan, Fiji — just look at the visitors' book.'

ESTABLISHED:	▶ 1828
TYPE:	▶ Manned
ENGINEER:	▶ Robert Stevenson
POSITION:	▶ 54° 38.1' N 4° 51.4' W at the most southerly point of Scotland
CHARACTER:	▶ Flashing white every 20 seconds
ELEVATION:	▶ 99 metres
NOMINAL RANGE:	▶ 28 miles
STRUCTURE:	▶ White round tower, 26 metres high
FOG SIREN:	▶ 2 blasts every 60 seconds

POINT OF AYRE

The climate is kind on the Isle of Man, even at its most northerly tip, the Point of Ayre. There are palm trees dotted around the lighthouse garden. The sheltered waters of the Irish Sea warmed by the Gulf Stream lap the long broad shingle beach below the tower and the place seems more akin to the Bahamas than the British Isles.

Assistant Keeper Ian McKay and his family came from Davaar, a rugged lump of an island, for the kinder peninsula. Ian's father had been a lightkeeper before him, but he resigned from the job when he was transferred to Skerryvore. 'He had had enough of isolation,' said Ian. 'On the rocks was six weeks duty and two weeks off in those days.

'I had asked the Board for a shift from Davaar,' said Ian, now Local Assistant at St Abb's Head. 'It wasn't the best place for a family.' He described how he and his wife Trish had stumbled across the Dhorlin, an umbilical cord of a shingle bar which connects the island to the mainland with each ebbing tide, when Trish was expecting their second child. A force 9 gale was blowing at the time. 'We had a taxi to meet at the mainland end of the Dhorlin, then a flight from Macrihanish to Glasgow for Trish to get to hospital to have the baby. Well, we had memories of that day, and so when Trish was expecting our third child we had to live somewhere that wasn't so remote so that's how we came to the Isle of Man, and four months after we arrived our daughter Mary was born.'

Trish made friends near the Point of Ayre when the children attended the local play school, and both Ian and Trish have fond memories of the Kirkbride school. 'I don't know how Mrs Brown, the head teacher, found enough hours in the day to do all the work with those children,' said Ian. 'Always doing projects — including one on the lighthouse. Our children came on really fast at that school with their reading and writing.'

'We like the lighthouse life,' said Trish McKay. 'We don't worry about all the bills we used to get before we joined the lighthouse service. There's just one problem really. The other assistant keeper and his family live in the house below us and they say we make too much noise unnecessarily. But we do try to be quiet, but we're a large family too. We just think Alec is too used to the real quiet and solitude you get on a rock.'

ESTABLISHED:	▶ 1818
TYPE:	▶ Manned
ENGINEER:	▶ Robert Stevenson
POSITION:	▶ 54° 24.9' N 4° 22.1' W at the most northerly point of the Isle of Man
CHARACTER:	▶ Alternate flashing white/red every 60 seconds
ELEVATION:	▶ 32 metres
NOMINAL RANGE:	▶ 19 miles
STRUCTURE:	▶ White tower with 2 red bands, 30 metres high
FOG SIREN:	▶ 3 blasts of 2.5 seconds every 90 seconds

Right, Local Assistant Douglas Ogden in the lantern. Left, Point of Ayre minor light nearby.

LANGNESS

'When Sule Skerry closed down my next station was Langness. I wasn't too pleased about it. On the ferry over here I was on the deck, and a Manxman spoke to me, "And we call you incomers," he said, "'comeovers'; you know, you'll like it here," so I said to him, "Listen, I'm no 'comeover', and I'm no 'stopover' either, 'cause I'm a 'sentover', and I won't like it." Keepers feel like the leftovers when they come here.' At first, Alistair MacDonald, now in his fourth year at Langness, missed Orkney very much. 'But you get used to the new places,' he said. 'Manx people are intensely proud of their island and rightly so, and they want you to be as impressed by it as they are.'

The Isle of Man's Ronaldsway Airport is less than two miles away, and there are about forty flights in and out each day in the summer. 'The postman was at the door soon after I arrived. "You'll like it here," he said, "it's very peaceful." I told him, "It's the noisiest station I have been at," but I don't notice the planes now, unless the odd one flies directly overhead.'

The well-manicured lighthouse helicopter pad is rarely used. 'In fact,' said Jimmy Burns, the Principal Keeper, 'I don't think it's ever been used.' Its sparkling white outlines are carefully maintained nevertheless. 'I gave it a coat of paint just last week,' said Alistair. Six geese help. Alistair bought them soon after arriving. 'They're not for the pot, they're pets on grass-cutting duties.'

Night school in Douglas for Alistair means that sometimes an evening class clashes with his watch duties, but cooperation among the keepers has ensured flexible arrangements for everyone's benefit. 'I've discovered an interest in maths I never knew I had. I'm doing an A-level course just now and a welding course too, and in my first year here I studied physics. They might help later if I want to become a mature student at college.

'It's Mad Sunday today, the first Sunday in the Isle of Man TT races, when the fans who come here from all over Europe with their own motorbikes show themselves off. You can hear them all in Douglas long before you get there — it's like a swarm of angry bees.'

ESTABLISHED:	▶ 1880
TYPE:	▶ Manned
ENGINEER:	▶ David and Thomas Stevenson
POSITION:	▶ 54° 3.5' N 4° 37.2' W, on south eastern coast of the Isle of Man
CHARACTER:	▶ Flashing 2 white every 30 seconds
NOMINAL RANGE:	▶ 21 miles
STRUCTURE:	▶ White tower, 19 metres high
FOG SIREN:	▶ 2 blasts every 60 seconds

CHICKEN ROCK

Hugh Cowley is a Port St Mary Commissioner. 'I went to the Chicken Rock in '54,' he said, 'to replace a sick keeper, he was ill with pleurisy. I went out for a day but had to stay for a week because of bad weather. I'd never been a lightkeeper before. It's the only time, that week. There was a little cupboard in the kitchen, on the fourth floor of the tower I think, which you opened to look at a cable that held a weight. It slowly descended the tower to turn the lens. When a red marker appeared on the cable in the cupboard then it was time to wind. We could see the light from the kitchen too; there was a little mirror jutting out from one of the windows which reflected the lantern.

'I got my ears clipped the first night I was out there, from the Principal Lightkeeper. I'd used two matches instead of one to light up with. At that time it was a paraffin light which had to be preheated with a meths flame for about ten minutes. Then a wax taper was used to transfer the flame to the mantle and ignite the paraffin vapour. That's where I used a second match instead of using the taper.

'I'd never have made a lightkeeper. I couldn't get the hang of using the fog signal. It was supposed to fire two explosives every five minutes. When I practised with it I could only get the contraption fixed up in twice that time. But luckily there was no fog anyway when I was out there.'

ESTABLISHED:	▶ 1875
TYPE:	▶ Major automatic (1961)
ENGINEER:	▶ David and Thomas Stevenson
POSITION:	▶ 54° 2.3' N 4° 50.1' W, off the southwest coast of the Isle of Man
CHARACTER:	▶ Flashing white every 5 seconds
ELEVATION:	▶ 38 metres
NOMINAL RANGE:	▶ 13 miles
STRUCTURE:	▶ Granite tower, 44 metres high
FOGHORN:	▶ 2 blasts every 60 seconds

ST ABB'S HEAD

A cluster of white houses surrounded by a white wall stand on top of
St Abb's Head. Three families live here. The tiny tower is tucked at the
bottom of a slope below the houses. This is one of only two stations
where the keepers go down to the light from their homes; the other is
Maughold Head, on the Isle of Man. Three times a day, St Abb's Head
calls the keepers at Bass Rock, Isle of May and Bell Rock on the radio,
and there is a constant monitoring of the automatic light on Fidra.

'When I first got word that I was to be stationed at St Abb's,' said
Jimmy Watt, Assistant Keeper, 'we drove over, me and the family. It
was September, and it began to rain on the way here, and it got dark.
We took the narrow, winding track for the last two miles, and rattled
over the cattle grids in the dark, and then drove up the last steep grind
up to the station. It wasn't the best way to see the place.'

'We get a lot of school parties here,' said Duncan Jordan, Principal
Keeper. 'I can't think of a single child who hasn't written a letter back
to say "thank you". One question they always ask is "How much does
the lightbulb cost?" That's the light in the tower. Well, I never knew
the answer until we had an engineer down from 84 one day. He said
they cost over £100 each, so I'll know the next time I'm asked.

'We had a visitor here a couple of years ago — he was a German —
who came in to tell me about what I thought was a ship on the rocks. I
was a bit startled. "No, no," he said, "not a ship, a sheep." Well, I got it
worked out eventually. But then he did talk about a ship — he'd been
shipwrecked as a boy on the rocks below here back in 1958, he said —
it's in the Shipwreck Return Book. Here it is. A motor vessel, the
Nyon. Ran ashore in dense fog and drizzle.'

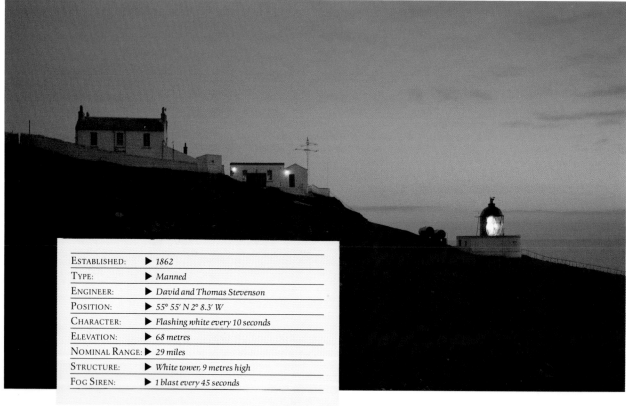

ESTABLISHED:	▶ 1862
TYPE:	▶ Manned
ENGINEER:	▶ David and Thomas Stevenson
POSITION:	▶ 55° 55′ N 2° 8.3′ W
CHARACTER:	▶ Flashing white every 10 seconds
ELEVATION:	▶ 68 metres
NOMINAL RANGE:	▶ 29 miles
STRUCTURE:	▶ White tower, 9 metres high
FOG SIREN:	▶ 1 blast every 45 seconds

BASS ROCK

'It's not a bad life out here. This is the fourth station I've been at. You can go for a walk here; we've got vegetable gardens, a workshop and good living quarters; enough to keep you occupied.' Kenny Weir tried some poetry once, he said. 'I took it home to the wife but she just laughed. Mind you, on the rock it sounded beautiful after a month. But ashore it sounded stupid. So I never did that again.

'When I first came into the job the Principal's word was law over everything. It's more democratic now. For instance, we come to some agreement over the food orders before we send it to the store. We don't eat macaroni every day just because the Principal likes macaroni.

'This is my third paraffin-lamp station,' said Kenny. 'I prefer the oil lamps; you can care for them, and you can repair them yourself. You don't know what you're doing with the electrical systems fitted in some towers. Yes, you have to carry paraffin up the tower here every day and pump the stuff during the night, and you can smell it too, but you don't care. You can't smell much out here after a while anyway, except the gannets.'

Calum MacAulay is the Principal of the Bass. He is from the Western Isles and is a quiet easy-going person. 'My hobby on the rocks is the kind of thing most people expect of lightkeepers. I make model ships and put them into these whisky bottles in my spare time.' A row of dimpled bottles lined the mantelpiece, each containing a ship sitting on a choppy blue sea with a background of blue sky and white clouds.

ESTABLISHED:	▶ 1902
TYPE:	▶ Manned
ENGINEER:	▶ D. Alan Stevenson
POSITION:	▶ 56° 4.6' N 2° 38.3' W, on an island lying 3 miles northeast of North Berwick
CHARACTER:	▶ Flashing 6 white every 30 seconds
ELEVATION:	▶ 46 metres
NOMINAL RANGE:	▶ 21 miles
STRUCTURE:	▶ White tower, 20 metres high
FOGHORN:	▶ 3 blasts at 4 second intervals every 2 minutes

INCHKEITH

As well as the ruins of an experimental light tower used in the 1840s, the island of Inchkeith is cluttered with the remains of war activity. There are derelict houses, gun emplacements and huge sheds. Underground corridors lead to bunkers and stores, the remnants of the many garrisons stationed here during the Napoleonic wars and more recently two World Wars in this century. Only the summit, where the lighthouse stands, is clear of the dereliction.

Davey Leslie, who was awarded the British Empire Medal in 1985, is the Principal Keeper. 'I started on the Bass Rock. The PLK said, "Can you cook, Davey?" I said, "No." He said, "Can you boil water?" I said, "Yes." He said, "You can cook." That was William Sinclair. He's still around Edinburgh. He must be well into his 80s.

'"When Davey goes," they say in the office, "that's another character gone." I dug out a garden below the tower. It was rough, but I grow potatoes, carrots, turnips, onions, cabbages. I had to build a barricade around it and cover the whole thing with nets to keep the gulls off. Thousands of gulls nest all over the island, the blackbacks and the herring gulls. I've got a greenhouse with tomatoes. When I'm ashore, the other Principal Keeper looks after it.'

ESTABLISHED:	▶ 1804
TYPE:	▶ Manned
ENGINEER:	▶ Thomas Smith
POSITION:	▶ 56° 2′ N 3° 8′ W, on an island in the Firth of Forth, 3 miles north of Edinburgh
CHARACTER:	▶ Flashing white every 15 seconds
ELEVATION:	▶ 70 metres
NOMINAL RANGE:	▶ 23 miles
STRUCTURE:	▶ Brown stone tower, 19 metres high, of architectural and historic interest
FOGHORN:	▶ 1 blast of 1.5 seconds every 15 seconds

Davey Leslie, BEM, Principal Keeper, centre, with Jimmy Jamieson, left, and Bob Byers, right.

ISLE OF MAY

'Traffic jam!' says Norrie Muir as he slows the tractor to a walking pace. An eider duck and four fluffy newly hatched ducklings are waddling along the track in front of him. In pockets of soft warm grey down eiders' eggs are hatching all over the island now, and delicate vulnerable chicks with anxious mothers are making their way over carpets of sea pinks and sea campion to the shore.

'We'll have to change this colour scheme. It makes us feel sick to look at this every day,' says Norrie as he looks around the lighthouse living room. The room has pale green walls and pale yellow woodwork. Just beyond the elegant almost ecclesiastical windows two wild rabbits and a herring gull are finishing off the kitchen scraps after the keepers' lunch.

There used to be four keepers here, an unusual number for a rock station. This was because two were needed to be on watch during fog, one to man the lighthouse and one to man the machinery for the two foghorns which have now been discontinued.

The lighthouse building — more of a castle than a tower — was built in 1816. To the east is the Low Light tower, established in 1844 as a second leading light for avoiding the North Carr rocks off the nearby Fife coast. It was discontinued in 1887 and the building is now used by birdwatchers.

ESTABLISHED:	▶ 1816
TYPE:	▶ Manned
ENGINEER:	▶ Robert Stevenson
POSITION:	▶ 56° 11.2' N 2° 33.3' W
CHARACTER:	▶ Flashing white every 20 seconds
ELEVATION:	▶ 73 metres
NOMINAL RANGE:	▶ 26 miles
STRUCTURE:	▶ Square tower on stone dwelling, 24 metres high, of architectural and historic interest

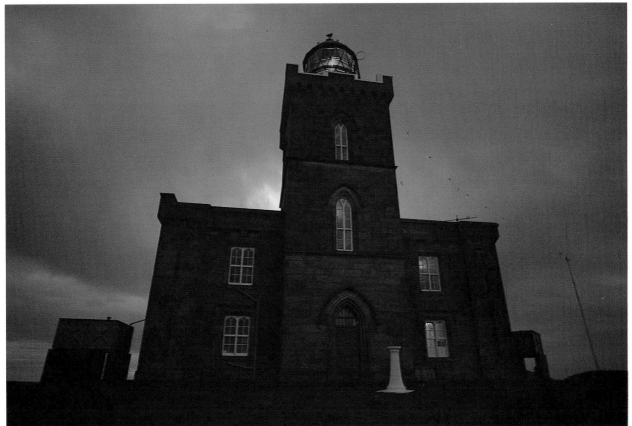

*Opposite, Jimmy Peoples, Relief Keeper.
Top left, Norrie Muir, Principal Keeper, left,
Jimmy Peoples, Raymond Allan and Bob
Stevenson, Local Assistants. Centre, The
former Low Light seen through a prism at the
main light. Bottom, lens and prisms.*

BELL ROCK

'It's a piece of cake around here,' said Captain Morrison on the bridge of the *Pharos*. 'After the seas around Orkney there's nothing to it.' The *Pharos* had made the run to the Bass Rock and the Isle of May with supplies and was now heading for Bell Rock to make the relief. Two men were to go on to the rock and two were to leave. 'We'll only use the helicopter if we really have to at the Bell,' said Captain Morrison, 'and that's not often. We usually get the launch in there.'

The *Pharos* anchored off the Bell and waited for the tide to fall. An hour later the launch was in the water, and the men and supplies were aboard. Two keepers hung on to the ladder below the lighthouse door, anxiously waiting to get on the grating which connects the lighthouse to the jetty. Suddenly the jetty cleared of water. The launch made for the landing, and the relief began. Gas cylinders, breakers of water, boxes of groceries and belongings were carried along the narrow grating to the tower. Waves burst over the men left in the launch, and swept the landing. Empty cylinders and boxes were thrown into the launch. With keepers and boatmen all aboard, the relief was over.

John Boath, one of the two Principal Keepers.

ESTABLISHED:	▶ 1811
TYPE:	▶ Manned
ENGINEER:	▶ Robert Stevenson
POSITION:	▶ 56° 26.1' N 2° 23.1' W, on submerged reef
CHARACTER:	▶ Flashing white every 3 seconds
NOMINAL RANGE:	▶ 28 miles
STRUCTURE:	▶ White tower, 36 metres high
FOGHORN:	▶ 2 blasts every 60 seconds

The Bell Rock Signal Tower at Arbroath, formerly the Shore Station, now a museum.

GIRDLE NESS

George Pearson, PLK, calls himself an old paraffin-oiler. He started when the lights were lit by paraffin, and he is now the longest serving keeper in Scotland. 'Thirty-nine years, this year,' he says. His brother, who joined the service soon after him, lives just twenty miles to the south, at Tod Head Lighthouse. 'I wish I was a supernumerary again,' says George. 'I would do it all over again. I would too.'

Aberdeen is less than a mile from the lighthouse. 'I have two Occasional Keepers here,' says George. 'They're both city men, both called George. We call them George the First and George the Second. They were retired, so this occasional work suits them.

'I'd rather be at Girdle Ness than anywhere. It's one of the best. It's great after Cape Wrath, and I was on the Bell for five years. No joy there, I can tell you.'

Top, Chris Smyth, Assistant Keeper, in the lantern. Above, Travelling Keeper Sam Neighbour and his wife Nadeje.

ESTABLISHED:	▶ 1833
TYPE:	▶ Manned
ENGINEER:	▶ Robert Stevenson
POSITION:	▶ 57° 8.3' N 2° 2.8' W, on headland at south entrance to Aberdeen harbour
CHARACTER:	▶ Flashing 2 every 20 seconds
NOMINAL RANGE:	▶ 22 miles
STRUCTURE:	▶ White round tower, 37 metres high, of architectural and historic interest
FOG SIREN:	▶ Every 60 seconds

KINNAIRD HEAD

Above, Principal Keeper James Shanks and his wife. Opposite, Local Assistant James Strachan in the lantern.

ESTABLISHED:	▶ 1787
TYPE:	▶ Manned
ENGINEER:	▶ Thomas Smith
POSITION:	▶ 57° 41.9' N 2° 0.1' W, on headland south of Fraserburgh
CHARACTER:	▶ Flashing white every 15 seconds
ELEVATION:	▶ 37 metres
NOMINAL RANGE:	▶ 25 miles
STRUCTURE:	▶ White tower, 23 metres high, of architectural and historic interest
FOGHORN:	▶ 1 blast of 7 seconds every 1.5 minutes

The first lighthouse to be built by the Northern Lighthouse Board was Kinnaird Head. The tower was built within the walls of an old castle and stands on the edge of the bustling fishing port of Fraserburgh. The castle itself is occasionally occupied by a travelling keeper or a supernumerary, while the Principal and his assistants and their families live in the Board's houses below the castle.

'This is my home for a few weeks,' said Jim Dalling, a supernumerary now in his sixth year as a keeper. His room in the castle was at the end of a passage which leads from a door halfway up the tower. It was a huge room with tall elegant windows, an old radio the size of a sideboard, a cooker, a bed and his own portable television set for use at shore stations.

Kinnaird Head is the control station for the automatic Rattray Head Lighthouse, a few miles to the south. Len Fraser was one of the last keepers at Rattray and is now at Holburn Head. 'After we left, a woman's voice used to automatically tell the keepers at Kinnaird what was happening in the lighthouse. The keeper on watch would phone the tower and the voice would go through a list and tell you whether the light had switched on or whether the foghorn was sounding, and all sorts of things. "Rachel" we used to call her. She was there before we left. Her voice would call out if anyone broke into the tower: it would be enough to scare anyone away. Then she was replaced by an American electronic voice. "Rachel ate the tapes" we used to say.'

COVESEA SKERRIES

The lighthouse at Covesea Skerries, which was lit in 1846, was automated in 1984 and its original lens moved to the Fisheries and Community Museum in Lossiemouth. The building, designed by Alan Stevenson, is listed as being of architectural and historic interest and is now available to staff of the Northern Lighthouse Board as a holiday home.

ESTABLISHED:	▶ 1846
TYPE:	▶ Major automatic (1984)
ENGINEER:	▶ Alan Stevenson
POSITION:	▶ 57° 43.5' N 3° 20.2' W
CHARACTER:	▶ Flashing white/red every 20 seconds
NOMINAL RANGE:	▶ White 24 miles, red 20 miles
STRUCTURE:	▶ White tower, 36 metres high, of architectural and historic interest

ESTABLISHED:	▶ 1830
TYPE:	▶ Major automatic (1985)
ENGINEER:	▶ Robert Stevenson
POSITION:	▶ 57° 51.9' N 3° 46.5' W
CHARACTER:	▶ Flashing 4 white every 30 seconds
NOMINAL RANGE:	▶ 24 miles
STRUCTURE:	▶ White tower, 41 metres high, with red bands; of architectural interest

TARBAT NESS

Jack Clark, now retired, was the last Principal Keeper of Tarbat Ness Lighthouse before it was automated in 1983. He did not like living amongst hills and mountains so he was glad to be back where it's flat. 'You can see for miles round here. We've just had five years at Ardnamurchan. You're right out on a limb there, with great mountains behind you. And what a road out there. I took the Land Rover sixty miles to Fort William and sixty miles back once a week for anyone at the light who wanted the shopping in the town. What a thingummy road. . . .'

Around the Tarbat Ness tower the lawns had erupted into a beautiful meadow of wild flowers and grasses. The lighthouse Flymo had broken down and the grass had not been cut for weeks. In the soft early morning sunlight a pair of redshanks called urgently from the white wall to their two tiny chicks which were struggling through the grass behind the keepers' houses. A letter H is stamped on the ground near the lighthouse road. It marks the helicopter pad, a closely cropped bed of heather dotted with delicate purple orchids and all encompassed within a white ring.

CAPE WRATH

The early January helicopter relief to Cape Wrath was beginning, although the weather was worsening. The relieving keepers arrived, and, once loaded, the helicopter took off from the airstrip of the nuclear power station at Dounreay, some 45 miles directly east of the Cape. A gale was raging, and the cloud layer was low. On the way a report to the pilot of gusts of over sixty knots at the Cape meant that he would have to land about two miles from the lighthouse.

The helicopter followed mile after mile of rough track over a wilderness of moors before landing near a Land Rover, where the keepers were waiting for us to appear. In the roar of the gale and the engine the exchange of crew was over in minutes. We clung to the sides of the Land Rover as the helicopter took off.

'Everything's gone wrong this time out. The tractor's out of action, the diesel engine generators are breaking down, and ten days ago lightning struck the station and put our telephone out of order. It blew a couple of holes in the ground near the flag pole,' reported Principal Keeper Bill Anderson, looking despondent after only two weeks at the Cape.

The wind dropped a little overnight and turned to the northwest. A telephone engineer was expected to cross the Kyle of Durness in the ferry, some twelve miles away, to repair the damaged line. Before it was turned into a rock station, the families had to depend on the ferry. And if it could not get back across the Kyle then they had to stay overnight in the village of Durness. The ferryman, John Muir, and his wife were loading the boat with some boxes of their belongings before crossing to collect the engineer. 'Every time we cross we take something with us,' said Mrs Muir. 'Eleven years we've been on the Cape; it's enough. We've been happy here, but we're happy to go now.'

ESTABLISHED:	▶ 1828
TYPE:	▶ Manned
ENGINEER:	▶ Robert Stevenson
POSITION:	▶ 58° 37.5′ N 5° W, at the northwest tip of mainland Scotland
CHARACTER:	▶ Flashing 4 white every 30 seconds
ELEVATION:	▶ 122 metres
NOMINAL RANGE:	▶ 24 miles
STRUCTURE:	▶ White tower, 20 metres high, of architectural and historic interest
FOG SIREN:	▶ 6-second blast every 90 seconds

DUNNET HEAD

The most northerly inhabitants of the British mainland are the keepers of the Dunnet Head Lighthouse and their families. The novelty of this fact attracts visitors from all over the world, who come to stare at the lighthouse and walk along the cliffs. The keeper on watch each afternoon in the summer months takes the visitors up the tower in groups to look at the great lenses, to hear a little of the history of the place, and on a clear day to view through the lantern the Pentland Firth and on its far side the great cliffs of Hoy in Orkney.

'They ask all kinds of questions,' said Allan Tulloch, a keeper from Orkney, 'and you try to explain that the light doesn't flash but that the beams sweep across the sea. And they don't really believe you when you tell them about the Firth being one of the world's most dangerous waters. They see it on a fine day and think it's a myth. "How does the foghorn work?" they ask. "Does it really work by sucking in all that fog?" "How do you sleep at night with the foghorn on?" two girls asked. They'd been camping some miles away, towards Thurso, and said they couldn't sleep all night with the noise. Well, we live just yards from the horn and don't hear it after a while.'

Even the Queen Mother mentioned the foghorn when she visited the lighthouse in 1978. She dropped in without warning with some friends from New Zealand one afternoon. They were all staying at the Queen Mother's home, the Castle of Mey, a few miles up the road. The Principal asked them in for tea, and they stayed for two hours. 'I can see seven lights from my home,' said the Queen Mother, 'but this is the first lightkeeper's house I've ever been in.'

ESTABLISHED:	▶ 1831
TYPE:	▶ Manned
ENGINEER:	▶ Robert Stevenson
POSITION:	▶ 58° 40.3′ N 3° 22.4′ W, at the most northerly point of mainland Scotland
CHARACTER:	▶ Flashing 4 white every 30 seconds
ELEVATION:	▶ 105 metres
NOMINAL RANGE:	▶ 26 miles
STRUCTURE:	▶ White stone tower, 20 metres high
FOG SIREN:	▶ 3 blasts every 90 seconds

STROMA

The Attending Boatman to the lighthouse on Stroma, off Scotland's north coast, is Jimmy Simpson who lives in Caithness on the mainland. Jimmy was about 14 when he and his family left Stroma for the mainland, then in 1960 he bought the island where he farms cattle and sheep. He has converted the two former churches, one Presbyterian and one Baptist, into farm storage sheds, and when he is on the island he stays in the Presbyterian church manse. As a child there in the 1930s and 40s Jimmy was one of almost 50 pupils in the island's school, but by the late 1950s the total population had fallen to 30 or 40 people, dwindling rapidly after the first few families left. Many of the young people left for work at Dounreay Nuclear Power Station, tempted by the large wages for construction work. Others moved to crofts in Caithness. When the young people left, then the old had to leave too eventually, although some struggled on as best they could. A new harbour was finished in 1956 but by 1958 there were only three or four pupils in the school. The last family left in 1962. 'They pulled the anchor and were away' says Jimmy Simpson.

The lighthouse on Stroma remained a shore station until 1961, when the families moved to Stromness. It is a rock station, so three keepers now live there alone doing their four-week spells of duty, followed by four weeks off. At their doorstep are the swirling waters of the Pentland Firth, and at each tide's ebbing the great whirlpool, the Swelkie of Stroma, roars beyond the shore. There are whirlpools around the shores of Stroma's neighbour, the little island of Swona, across the Firth. These are the Wells of Swona. Sir Walter Scott sailed through the Pentland Firth on the Lighthouse Board's 1814 Inspection Tour, and he referred to Stroma and Swona as 'two wicked little islands'. He knew well how easy it was to be drawn on to the rocks around the islands by the tides of the Firth, and even today it is one of the world's most dangerous seaways.

ESTABLISHED:	▶ 1896
TYPE:	▶ Manned
ENGINEER:	▶ David A. Stevenson
POSITION:	▶ 58° 41.8′ N 3° 7′ W, on island in the Pentland Firth 3.5 miles northwest of Duncansby Head
CHARACTER:	▶ Flashing 2 white every 20 seconds
ELEVATION:	▶ 32 metres
NOMINAL RANGE:	▶ 26 miles
STRUCTURE:	▶ White tower, 23 metres high
FOGHORN:	▶ 2 blasts every 60 seconds

PENTLAND SKERRIES

By a stone wall, in the middle of the island of Muckle Skerry and not far from the Pentland Skerries Lighthouse, lies one of Scotland's loneliest graves. It is here that seven of the crew of the *Vicksburg,* a barque carrying coal from Leith to Quebec, were buried after being shipwrecked and drowned on the west point of the island in 1884. Below the same stone lie the graves of the two children of a lightkeeper. The lighthouse is a rock station now, and the keepers are the island's only inhabitants.

The Shipwreck Return Book of the Pentland Skerries Lighthouse records many other wrecks on the islands over the years. In June 1871, John Brown, Principal Lightkeeper, wrote of the wreck of the *Good Desire:* '. . . the vessel became unmanageable, the crew then left her with the Boat . . . the Boat swamped and the crew all disappeared except two, one man and a boy. . . . The boy got hold of two of the boat's oars and drifted round to the East side of the island when Mr Montgomery, Assistant Keeper, swam in with a rope and got hold of him and saved him. The man drifted away with the tide. . . . The attending boatman, Mr Budge, never seed anything of the man that drifted past the island on the boat's bottom.'

For over a hundred years the Budge family provided the attending boatmen to the Pentland Skerries. The tradition ended in 1955, but the Attending Boatman now, as then, lives on South Ronaldsay.

In 1977 the USS *Pioneer Commander* of the US Navy ran aground on a submerged skerry off the island. She was floated off after a week with the assistance of a Dutch tug.

ESTABLISHED:	▶ 1794
TYPE:	▶ Manned
ENGINEER:	▶ Thomas Smith and Robert Stevenson
POSITION:	▶ 58° 41.4' N 2° 55.4' W
CHARACTER:	▶ Flashing 3 white every 30 seconds
NOMINAL RANGE:	▶ 25 miles
STRUCTURE:	▶ White tower, 36 metres high, of architectural and historic interest
FOGHORN:	▶ 1 blast of 7 seconds every 90 seconds

SWONA

Pitiful crying pierced the murmur of the sea and the wind. It was like the sound made by human babies and came from the shore below the island's schoolhouse, but it was the silvery sleepy pups of a small colony of grey seals.

James Rosie had returned for just a day to the island that had been his home until 1974. He had lived here with his brother and sister, but then his brother died so James moved across the water to South Ronaldsay with his sister. No one lives on Swona now. Even the old tower has gone, replaced in 1983 by a modern concrete structure.

In the doorway of the school by the Swona shore James Rosie, old and frail and full of island memories, looked at the empty room. 'I sat on that bench,' he said. 'We'd take it in turns every few minutes to sit on the end nearest the fireplace during the lessons.' He was looking back over half a century. Since the last teacher left, a Bible has lain on the mantelpiece.

A photograph of the *Pennyslvania* hangs in the sitting room of James Rosie's cottage. This ship struck Swona in June 1931 in dense fog. The first thing the islanders knew of it was when the ship's first mate knocked on James' door at 5 o'clock in the morning. The *Pennyslvania* was only one of many ships to have been wrecked on Swona. Some have struck so hard that the islanders have felt the shudder in their homes and the crash has been heard as far away as South Ronaldsay. One ship struck the south end of Swona so hard that all kinds of things were flung off the deck and on to the island, including what looked like red-lead paint scattered over the rocks.

Behind the house was a long shed containing all the flotsam and jetsam of many years of shipwreck and beachcombing. It was an Aladdin's cave, the walls and ceiling festooned with the sea's treasures, and among it all a sturdy clinker-built boat laden with gear. In the far corner of the shed was a Heath Robinson contraption. 'This is our old generator,' said James, topping it up with oil. He turned a handle sharply, and the machine burst into life at full throttle. A barrel of water soon bubbled and steamed — the cooling system — and on a board hanging above the engine the amps and voltage meters flickered.

'We used to get a call from the Duncansby Head lightkeepers when we lived here,' said James. 'We'd got an old radio set in 1950 through the *Exchange and Mart*. The keepers didn't need to call us because I was just Attendant Keeper to the automatic light.'

The Swona light has always been automatic. It is one of the minor lights of the Pentland Firth, but out of concern and kindness James was called by the Duncansby keepers just across the Firth every day when they made their routine calls to the other rock stations in the region. 'It was always handy in case of emergency,' said James, 'and anyway it was good to have a chat with someone else for a change.'

'I couldn't go back to Swona,' said Eva Annal, another of James's sisters, married to Sandy and living on South Ronaldsay. She was born and brought up on the island. 'There are too many ghosts there now.'

ESTABLISHED:	▶	1906
TYPE:	▶	Built as a minor automatic light
POSITION:	▶	58° 44.2' N 3° 4.1' W, on an island in the Pentland Firth, southwest of South Ronaldsay
CHARACTER:	▶	Flashing white every 8 seconds
ELEVATION:	▶	17 metres
NOMINAL RANGE:	▶	9 miles
STRUCTURE:	▶	White concrete column, 6 metres high, replacing previous tower in 1983

COPINSAY

Four great booms from the old foghorn were sounding every minute into the mist which had crept over Orkney since the afternoon. It was now late evening. The light was on at the lighthouse but was sending sweeping white shafts only yards into the darkness. In the sitting room, the windows rattled, the television picture disappeared, and the grandfather clock wobbled with each bellow.

'The man on watch sits in this chair,' said Murdoch Lamont, the Principal Lightkeeper, now at Neist Point, pointing to an armchair by a glowing coal fire. 'With a glance up there,' he said, flicking his eyes to a small mirror above the window, 'you can check the light from here. And the quickest way to the tower is out of the window — every forty-five minutes to wind the machine and pump the paraffin. We'll be electric here before long. Then the next step is for the station to be demanned. There'll be no one on the island then.'

Originally, the keepers lived at the lighthouse with their wives and children. A school teacher also lived on the island and had a classroom in the only farmhouse. Since then the farm has been deserted and the lighthouse designated a rock station, where the three keepers work their four weeks on and four weeks off. The shore station is in Stromness on Mainland Orkney, and usually, once a year, the families take a boat to the island for a day to visit their husbands.

Copinsay is now a Royal Society for the Protection of Birds nature reserve and in 1973 was dedicated to the memory of the late James Fisher, author, broadcaster and ornithologist. A little ceremony was held that year at the farmhouse by some of James Fisher's family and friends and the three lightkeepers and their attending boatmen. The speeches were made in the open air near the farmhouse, and periodically the voices were drowned as crowds of calling kittiwakes rose from the bay and spread along the shore. A plaque was placed on the side of the house:

> 'Storms there the stacks thrashed,
> there answered them the tern with icy feathers;
> full oft the erne wailed round spray-feathered. . . .'

ESTABLISHED:	▶ 1915
TYPE:	▶ Manned
ENGINEER:	▶ David Stevenson
POSITION:	▶ 58° 53.8' N 2° 40.2' W, on small island to the east of Orkney mainland
CHARACTER:	▶ Flashing 5 white every 30 seconds
ELEVATION:	▶ 79 metres
NOMINAL RANGE:	▶ 21 miles
STRUCTURE:	▶ White tower, 16 metres high
FOG SIREN:	▶ 4 blasts every 60 seconds

HOY HIGH AND HOY LOW

Tommy Thomson is a North Ronaldsay man. During his years as a keeper in the service he was stationed on Graemsay at Hoy High Lighthouse. While he was there the light was automated and demanned, and Tommy was able to buy one of the two lighthouse cottages. He continues to live there now with his family, and is Attendant Keeper to the two Graemsay lights, Hoy High and Hoy Low, and runs his croft of cattle and sheep including several of the unique breed of North Ronaldsay sheep.

Ronnie Mowatt and his wife live on a croft at the other side of Graemsay, by Hoy Sound. Ronnie was the Occasional Keeper to Hoy Low Lighthouse, and he is descended from an Irish foreman who stayed and married on Graemsay after he and his workmen had built the lighthouse in 1851.

On the shore below Hoy Low Lighthouse there lie the sea-worn remnants of crockery and bricks. They were part of the cargo of a ship which ran aground here during a terrible storm of gales and blizzards on 1 January 1866. The ship was the *Albion*, and a gravestone in the island's churchyard is a poignant reminder of the tragedy. Ronnie's cottage has some of the ship's cargo. His sideboard has a display of some of the large thick plates and bowls which survived the wreck.

ESTABLISHED:	▶ 1851
TYPE:	▶ Major automatic (Hoy High 1978, Hoy Low 1966)
ENGINEER:	▶ Alan Stevenson
POSITION:	▶ 58° 56.5' N 3° 18.4' W, on the Orkney island of Graemsay, Hoy High at northeast, Hoy Low at northwest
CHARACTER:	▶ Hoy High occulting white/red every 8 seconds; Hoy Low isophase white every 3 seconds
ELEVATION:	▶ Hoy High 35 metres, Hoy Low 17 metres
NOMINAL RANGE:	▶ Hoy High white 20 miles, red 16 miles; Hoy Low 15 miles
STRUCTURE:	▶ Hoy High white tower 33 metres high; Hoy Low, white tower 12 metres high

SULE SKERRY

Seals once thronged Sule Skerry, as the name 'Sule' suggests, but then the lighthouse was built on the island in the 1890s and with all the disturbance most of them dispersed to other islands in Orkney and to the remote islands far to the west, Sula Sgier and North Rona. With the absence of seals, much of the island's thirty-five acres was very quickly taken over each summer by tens of thousands of puffins. The ground, mostly a shallow light soil, surrounded by the island's rocky perimeter, is an ideal habitat for puffins, and the birds soon riddled Sule Skerry with a honeycomb of burrows and nests.

The number of puffins increased so dramatically that one of the island's first lightkeepers, James Tomison, wrote of them: '. . . it might be called *the* bird of the island, and in May and June one would be inclined to think that all the Tammies in the world made Sule Skerry their headquarters. . . . The air is black with them, the ground covered with them, every hole is tenanted with them. . . .'

The summers are brief on Sule Skerry. The paradise it might seem then is soon over, and the myriads of sea birds vanish. The first storm of early autumn changes the vegetation from green to brown overnight with wind blast and salt spray. For most of the year the island is a bleak and windswept place.

In 1982, eighty-seven years after the light was lit for the first time, Sule Skerry Lighthouse was fully automated and demanned. One of the last three keepers on the rock, Alistair MacDonald, had been Assistant there for five years. 'There's no keeper in Scotland that'll be sorry to see this place closed,' he said.

Perhaps the seals will return to swarm over Sule Skerry, their ancient home, now that the last lightkeepers have departed. The island might again become the island of seals, as described in legend and in the ballad, 'the Grey Selkie of Sule Skerrie':

> 'I am a man upon the land,
> And I'm a selkie on the sea,
> And when I'm far and far from land,
> My home it is on Sule Skerrie.'

Above, Arctic tern. Opposite top right, John Kermode, a PLK before automation, with anemometer.

'I can't stand it out here. I've got to get away!' cried one of the two workmen at the lighthouse. They had been flown out from Stromness to do some bricklaying as part of the alterations before the station was demanned. Within about three hours the younger of the two was in despair. The weather had worsened, with heavy showers of rain, and visibility was down to about four miles. On the radio transmitter to Headquarters he tried to explain how frightening it was for him. 'But you're on an island,' came the reply from Edinburgh. 'You've got some land around you. You're not stuck in a tower.'

'Have a brandy?' asked the Assistant Keeper as he brought a small bottle out of the medical box.

'No, no, I don't drink,' was the reply.

'Oh, it's just as well. This is weak tea in here. Someone's been at the brandy.'

A helicopter was summoned from Aberdeen, and on advice over the radio from the doctor in Stromness the distressed workman was subdued with Mogadon. As darkness was beginning to close in, around 8 p.m., the helicopter arrived, and about twenty minutes later the workman was landed back at Stromness. Willy, his partner, stayed on. 'I'll finish the job on my own,' he said calmly, 'even if it does take twice as long.'

Ronnie Leask from Orkney, now Local Assistant at Stroma, was on Sule Skerry before it was automated. 'Sule Skerry closed, boy, a couple of years ago. Well, we had a travelling keeper with us out there for a fortnight. He was an English lad, and his first week he was the cook.

ESTABLISHED:	▶ 1895
TYPE:	▶ Major automatic (1982)
ENGINEER:	▶ David A. Stevenson
POSITION:	▶ 59° 5' N 4° 24.3' W, on island 37 miles west of Orkney and 45 miles northwest of Dunnet Head
CHARACTER:	▶ Flashing 2 white every 15 seconds
ELEVATION:	▶ 34 metres
NOMINAL RANGE:	▶ 19 miles
STRUCTURE:	▶ White tower, 27 metres high, of architectural and historic interest

Well, boy, boy, I'll never forget it. He had made the most enormous lemon meringue pie — great clouds of meringue on top. Andy Sinclair was the Principal, he was an Orkneyman too, and he said to the travelling keeper, "Boy, what a tea we'll have." And later at tea time Andy took a slice and said, "But we've no eggs with us out here this time." "I made it with gulls' eggs, the blackbacks," said the travelling keeper. So Andy suddenly stood up, picked up the great pie and flung it out of the kitchen window. The kitchen was way up the tower in those days. Well, that pie went sailing down and splattered all over the steps below, and I'll tell you, boy oh boy, it was the gulls that had a rare tea that afternoon.'

BROUGH OF BIRSAY

The *Orkneyinga Saga* tells of the murder of Earl Magnus, one of
Orkney's 12th-century rulers, on Egilsay, and his subsequent burial in
a church, Orkney's first cathedral, on a tiny tidal island called the
Brough of Birsay. The ruins of this church can still be seen on the
slopes of the sea-pink carpeted island, and it was to Magnus' grave
that many people began to make pilgrimages. He became revered as a
saint and a martyr, and about twenty years later, his nephew,
Earl Rognvald, began the building of Kirkwall Cathedral, later called
St Magnus Cathedral where the remains of St Magnus were placed in a
cavity near the top of one of the pillars.

'I used to carry the gas cylinders on my back across the Brough,'
says Benny Norquoy, Attendant Keeper to the Brough of Birsay light.
'Some job I can tell you, boy,' he says. 'They were smaller than the
ones we use now. A helicopter delivers the new cylinders right to the
lighthouse door. It's the only light on the West Mainland except for
the Noup on Westray,' says Benny. 'The light was modernized in
1983; the lens is now only a fraction of the size of the original optics,
but its power is much greater.'

Benny Norquoy lives with his family in the small village opposite
the Brough, less than a mile from the lighthouse. 'The light flashes in
my bedroom every night,' says Benny. 'It's handy to keep a check on
it. I work on the *Orcadia*, the North Isles boat. Home every night,
boy. The fireside sailors, they call us.' He has thirty lobster creels
around the Brough, and he also fishes for haddock and cuithes with a
hand-line, the traditional way, in the summer months. The fish hang
outside his house to dry before storing. 'Good fun on a bonny night,'
he says.

ESTABLISHED:	▶ 1925
TYPE:	▶ Built as a major automatic light
POSITION:	▶ 59° 8.2' N 3° 20.3' W, on small tidal island off northwest Mainland Orkney
CHARACTER:	▶ Flashing 3 white every 25 seconds
ELEVATION:	▶ 52 metres
NOMINAL RANGE:	▶ 18 miles
STRUCTURE:	▶ White castellated tower and building, 11 metres high

145

START POINT

'I first came to Sanday with my brother,' said Mrs Scott. 'He was a keeper at the lighthouse here, and I lived with him. My brother moved on, of course. He got a shift, but I stayed, and I got married here.

'When I was courting I'd sometimes get back to the lighthouse quite late,' she recalled. 'I'd have to wait for the tide to be right, you see, before I could walk across the causeway.' She smiled. 'Sometimes, on a really dark night, and my brother was expecting me, he'd stop the lens turning in the lighthouse to shine a beam over the causeway so I could see my way over the stones and seaweed.

'I used to give the machine a wind when my brother was on watch, too. I'd dash up the stairs, give a quick check over things, give the handle all the turns it needed to get the weight to the top, and dash down again in no time.

'But I was to stay on Sanday, and my brother moved on, and I've lived here at Sparrowhall with my husband running the farm ever since.'

The lighthouse was automated and demanned in 1962. Since then the attendant keeper has been Andrew Skea who also runs Rusness Post Office at the north end of the island. The keepers' houses below the tower are empty now, and the windows are boarded over. The garden is overgrown, and the sundial has been removed from its plinth. The ancient Maesry tomb nearby, where the lightkeepers once stored their potatoes in its dark and cool chamber, has had its entrance blocked by a fall of stones.

ESTABLISHED:	▶ *1806*
TYPE:	▶ *Major automatic (1962)*
ENGINEER:	▶ *Thomas Smith and Robert Stevenson*
POSITION:	▶ *59° 16.7′ N 2° 22.5′ W, at eastern point of the Orkney Island of Sanday*
CHARACTER:	▶ *Flashing 2 white every 20 seconds*
ELEVATION:	▶ *24 metres*
NOMINAL RANGE:	▶ *19 miles*
STRUCTURE:	▶ *White tower, 23 metres high, with black vertical stripes*

FAIR ISLE

Golf is a popular pastime amongst many lightkeepers, who will sometimes create their own course if one does not already exist at their station. A course was soon created at the Fair Isle South Lighthouse, and Norrie Muir, the Principal Lightkeeper, described his efforts in the *Lighthouse* journal: 'The next thing was to make some holes and get some flags. We found that steam pudding tins were just the thing for the holes, so we had to eat our way through six tins of steam puddings, and keep on eating them, as they did not last long. If I ever see a tin of steam pudding again it will be too soon. Now for the flags. We found that broom handles were just the thing to put the flags on, and that is what we did. I have to admit that it made sweeping the engine-room floor difficult as we had to get down on our hands and knees. Now the Superintendent will know why I order so many brooms. . . .'

A golf tournament soon started between the keepers of Fair Isle South and those of Fair Isle North through the summer months, and they played for the Fair Isle Lightkeepers' Trophy.

'I was on Fair Isle when it was a shore station — it was about the most remote I've been to. There are only about sixty people on the island, and you only had your normal leave, and it's a long way to the mainland. It was too remote as a shore station. But now it's a rock station it's probably about the best in the service.'

ESTABLISHED:	▶ *1892*
TYPE:	▶ *Major automatic (1981)*
ENGINEER:	▶ *David A. Stevenson*
POSITION:	▶ *59° 33.2' N 1° 36.5' W*
CHARACTER:	▶ *Flashing 2 white every 30 seconds*
NOMINAL RANGE:	▶ *22 miles*
STRUCTURE:	▶ *White tower, 14 metres high*
FOGHORN:	▶ *3 blasts of 1.5 seconds every 45 seconds*

ESTABLISHED:	▶ 1892
TYPE:	▶ Manned
ENGINEER:	▶ David A. Stevenson
POSITION:	▶ 59° 30.9' N 1° 39' W
CHARACTER:	▶ Flashing 4 white every 40 seconds
NOMINAL RANGE:	▶ 24 miles
STRUCTURE:	▶ White tower, 26 metres high
FOG SIREN:	▶ 2 blasts every 60 seconds

SUMBURGH HEAD

Andy Flaws, Occasional Keeper at Sumburgh Head Lighthouse, makes superb model boats, a tradition in the lighthouse service, if a dying one. In the living room of the house of Assistant Keeper Jimmy Leask and his wife Eilean at Sumburgh Head hangs a photograph of a South Georgia whaling station. 'My father was a whaler until 1963,' says Jimmy. 'He was away whaling for about half the year every year in the South Atlantic. He was based in South Georgia, a flenser by the time he finished. Me, I was a baker in Lerwick, then took a job with the lights just before the bakery closed down.'

It is January, and Jimmy, being a Shetlander, has been involved with the annual Shetland fire festival, Up Helly Aa. Since becoming a lightkeeper, he has been able to attend the festival only once, in 1973, as he has been stationed at lighthouses away from Shetland. 'This year our squad was in the Guiser Jarl squad. We worked in the galley and made over eight hundred torches for the procession. We spent a year building the galley, then to see it set on fire.'

ESTABLISHED:	▶ 1821
TYPE:	▶ Manned
ENGINEER:	▶ Robert Stevenson
POSITION:	▶ 59° 51.3′ N 1° 16.3′ W
CHARACTER:	▶ Flashing 3 white every 30 seconds
FOG SIREN:	▶ 1 blast every 90 seconds

OUT SKERRIES

Lawrence Anderson was an occasional keeper and later fulltime at Out Skerries during the Second World War and recalls two unusual incidents. 'One of the keepers went up to the lightroom at midnight, then came rushing down and asked me to come up on the balcony where I would see something odd. I thought it might be some wartime activity, but I saw nothing. "Put your hand outside the rail" he said. When I did, there appeared to be jets of fire from every fingertip, similar to flames from a primus stove. When I looked at my companion, it was as if every hair on his head was on fire. The light was not on that night as it was wartime, and it must have been St Elmo's Fire.

'One very stormy day, the Principal Keeper and I were cleaning the lenses, inside the lantern, when we saw a vessel in distress. Its engines were running, but only its stern was above water and it was making slow progress stern first. It was a Norwegian MTB. Two of the men got ashore for help. At the first home they come to, the man of the house not recognizing the uniform, thought they were German. They asked him where the Post Office was. He answered, "I will not!" It was understandable as his mother had been killed when the shore station was bombed, but it was amusing too, as with the island being so small it would not have taken them long to find it anyway. All the crew were taken in to the homes and given food, dry clothes and a much needed bed.'

ESTABLISHED:	▶ 1854
TYPE:	▶ Major automatic (1972)
ENGINEER:	▶ David and Thomas Stevenson
POSITION:	▶ 60° 25.5' N 0° 43.5' W, on Bound Skerry, one of the Out Skerries group of islands, 5 miles northeast of Whalsay, Shetland
CHARACTER:	▶ Flashing white every 20 seconds
ELEVATION:	▶ 44 metres
NOMINAL RANGE:	▶ 20 miles
STRUCTURE:	▶ White tower, 30 metres high
FOGHORN:	▶ 2 blasts every 45 seconds

MUCKLE FLUGGA

Blizzards were sweeping across the north of Scotland and the northern isles, yet the mid-January helicopter relief was made at Muckle Flugga Lighthouse, on Shetland's northern tip.

'It took us three attempts to get to the Flugga that day,' said the helicopter pilot, Captain Phil Green. 'Twice we were forced back to land at the shore station.'

The shore station, the homes of the Muckle Flugga keepers and their families, is on a little promontory on Unst, the island to the south of the lighthouse island. Muckle Flugga is Britain's most northerly island, except for the wave-washed fragment called Out Stack, a few hundred yards beyond. These islands are farther north than Greenland's southern headlands and are only two hundred miles from Norway.

'It's not the storms and snow that are the main problems for our flights around Scotland, it's usually fog that can hold us up,' said the pilot. The helicopter, a five-seater including the two seats for the pilot and his navigator, seemed a fragile and vulnerable machine for traversing the vast stormswept waters around Scotland's remotest islands. 'The worst incident was out at Skerryvore,' he said. 'A freak wave swept over the helicopter soon after it landed on the rock at low water. It became a write-off in seconds.'

ESTABLISHED:	▶ *1854*
TYPE:	▶ *Manned*
ENGINEER:	▶ *Thomas and David Stevenson*
POSITION:	▶ *60° 51.3' N 0° 53' W, on small island off the north coast of Unst, Shetland*
CHARACTER:	▶ *Flashing 2 white every 20 seconds*
ELEVATION:	▶ *66 metres*
NOMINAL RANGE:	▶ *25 miles*
STRUCTURE:	▶ *White tower, 20 metres high*

THE NORTHERN LIGHTS

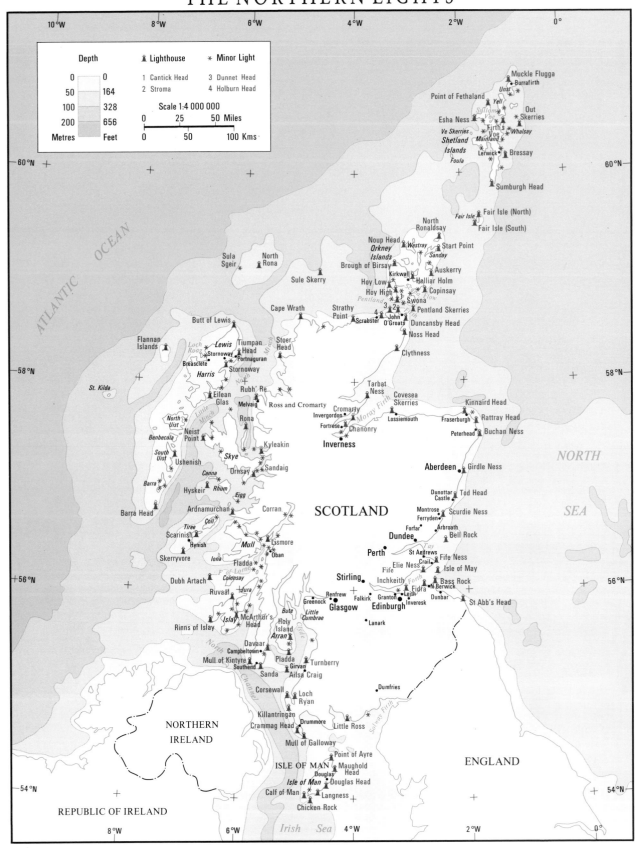

Depth

Metres	Feet
0	0
50	164
100	328
200	656

🛉 Lighthouse   ✳ Minor Light

1 Cantick Head   3 Dunnet Head
2 Stroma   4 Holburn Head

Scale 1:4 000 000

0   25   50 Miles
0   50   100 Kms

10°W   8°W   6°W   4°W   2°W   0°

60°N   60°N

58°N   58°N

56°N   56°N

54°N   54°N

ATLANTIC OCEAN

NORTH SEA

SCOTLAND

NORTHERN IRELAND

REPUBLIC OF IRELAND

ENGLAND

Irish Sea

Muckle Flugga, Burrafirth, Unst, Point of Fethaland, Out Skerries, Esha Ness, Ve Skerries, Firths Voe, Whalsay, Shetland Islands, Mainland, Lerwick, Bressay, Foula, Sumburgh Head, Fair Isle (North), Fair Isle (South), Fair Isle, North Ronaldsay, Start Point, Noup Head, Westray, Sanday, Orkney Islands, Brough of Birsay, Auskerry, Kirkwall, Helliar Holm, Hoy Low, Copinsay, Hoy High, Swona, Pentland Skerries, Strathy Point, Scrabster, John O'Groats, Duncansby Head, Cape Wrath, Noss Head, Clyness, Sula Sgeir, North Rona, Sule Skerry, Tarbat Ness, Covesea Skerries, Kinnaird Head, Butt of Lewis, Tiumpan Head, Stoer Head, Flannan Islands, Lewis, Stornoway, Portnaguran, Cromarty, Invergordon, Lossiemouth, Fraserburgh, Rattray Head, Breasclete, Harris, Portnaguran, Rubh' Re, Ross and Cromarty, Fortrose, Chanonry, Peterhead, Buchan Ness, St. Kilda, Eilean Glas, Melvaig, Inverness, North Uist, Rona, Benbecula, Neist Point, Kyleakin, Aberdeen, Girdle Ness, South Uist, Skye, Sandaig, Ushenish, Ornsay, Canna, Rhum, Dunottar Castle, Tod Head, Barra, Hyskeir, Eigg, Corran, Montrose, Scurdie Ness, Barra Head, Ardnamurchan, Ferryden, Coll, Tiree, Lismore, Forfar, Arbroath, Scarinish, Hynish, Oban, Dundee, Bell Rock, Skerryvore, Iona, Fladda, Perth, St Andrews, Crail, Fife Ness, Dubh Artach, Colonsay, Fife, Elie Ness, Isle of May, Ruvaal, Jura, Stirling, Inchkeith, Fidra, N Berwick, Islay, McArthur's Head, Renfrew, Falkirk, Granton, Leith, Bass Rock, Rinns of Islay, Bute, Holy Island, Greenock, Glasgow, Edinburgh, Inveresk, Dunbar, St Abb's Head, Little Cumbrae, Arran, Lanark, Davaar, Campbeltown, Pladda, Turnberry, Mull of Kintyre, Southend, Sanda, Girvan, Ailsa Craig, Corsewall, Loch Ryan, Dumfries, Killantringan, Crammag Head, Drummore, Little Ross, Solway Firth, Mull of Galloway, Point of Ayre, ISLE OF MAN, Maughold Head, Douglas, Isle of Man, Douglas Head, Calf of Man, Langness, Chicken Rock

MAJOR AUTOMATIC AND MANNED LIGHTHOUSES

WEST

NORTH RONA: *Major automatic built 1984*
Position: *59°07.3′N 5°48.8′W*
Character: *Flashing 3 white every 20 seconds*
Nominal range: *24 miles*
Structure: *White square tower 9 metres high*

FLANNAN ISLANDS: *See page 74*

BUTT OF LEWIS: *Manned, lit 1862*
Position: *58°31′N 6°15.7′W*
Character: *Flashing white every 5 seconds*
Nominal range: *25 miles*
Structure: *Redbrick tower 37 metres high*
Foghorn: *2 blasts every 30 seconds*

STOER HEAD: *See page 78*

TIUMPAN HEAD: *Major automatic (1985) lit 1900*
Position: *58°15.6′N 6°08.3′W*
Character: *Flashing 2 white every 30 seconds*
Nominal range: *24 miles*
Structure: *White tower 21 metres high*

STORNOWAY: *Major automatic (1963) lit 1852*
Position: *58°11.5′N 6°22.2′W*
Character: *Flashing white/red every 10 seconds*
Nominal range: *White 19 miles, red 15 miles*
Structure: *White round tower 14 metres high*

RUBH' RE: *Major automatic (1986) lit 1912*
Position: *57°51.4′N 5°48.6′W*
Character: *Flashing 4 white every 15 seconds*
Nominal range: *23 miles*
Structure: *White tower 25 metres high*

EILEAN GLAS: *See page 76*

SOUTH RONA: *Major automatic*
Position: *57°34.7′N 5°57.5′W*
Character: *Flashing white every 12 seconds*
Nominal range: *19 miles*
Structure: *White tower 13 metres high*

NEIST POINT: *See page 80*

USHENISH: *Major automatic (1970) lit 1857*
Position: *57°17.9′N 7°11.5′W*
Character: *Flashing white/red every 20 seconds*
Nominal range: *White 19 miles, red 15 miles*
Structure: *White tower 12 metres high*

ORNSAY: *See page 82*

HYSKEIR: *Manned, lit 1904*
Position: *56°58.2′N 6°40.9′W*
Character: *Flashing 3 white every 30 seconds*
Nominal range: *24 miles*
Structure: *White tower 39 metres high*

BARRA HEAD: *Major automatic (1980) lit 1833*
Position: *56°47.1′N 7°39.2′W*
Character: *Flashing white every 15 seconds*
Nominal range: *21 miles*
Structure: *White stone tower 18 metres high*

ARDNAMURCHAN: *See page 86*

SCARINISH: *Major automatic*
Position: *56°30′N 6°48.2′W*
Character: *Flashing white every 3 seconds*
Nominal range: *16 miles*
Structure: *White square tower 3 metres high*

LISMORE: *Major automatic (1965) lit 1833*
Position: *56°27.4′N 5°36.4′W*
Character: *Flashing white every 10 seconds*
Nominal range: *19 miles*
Structure: *White tower 26 metres high*

SKERRYVORE: *See page 88*

DUBH ARTACH: *See page 90*

RUVAAL: *Major automatic (1983) lit 1859*
Position: *55°56.2′N 6°07.3′W*
Character: *Flashing 3 white/red every 15 seconds*
Nominal range: *White 24 miles, red 21 miles*
Structure: *White tower 34 metres high, of architectural and
historic interest*

MCARTHUR'S HEAD: *Major automatic (1969) lit 1861*
Position: *55°45.9′N 6°02.8′W*
Character: *Flashing 2 white/red every 10 seconds*
Nominal range: *White 14 miles, red 11 miles*
Structure: *White tower 13 metres high*

RINNS OF ISLAY: *Manned, lit 1825*
Position: *55°40.4′N 6°30.8′W*
Character: *Flashing white every 5 seconds*
Nominal range: *24 miles*
Structure: *White tower 29 metres high*
Fog siren: *3 blasts every 90 seconds*

MULL OF KINTYRE: *See page 94*

SANDA: *Manned, lit 1850*
Position: *55°16.5′N 5°34.9′W*
Character: *Long flashing white/red every 24 seconds*
Nominal range: *White 19 miles, red 16 miles*
Structure: *White tower 15 metres high*
Fog siren: *1 blast of 7 seconds every 60 seconds*

DAVAAR: *Major automatic (1983) lit 1854*
Position: *55°25.7′N 5°32.4′W*
Character: *Flashing 2 white every 10 seconds*
Nominal range: *23 miles*
Structure: *White tower of architectural and historic interest*
Fog siren: *2 blasts every 20 seconds*

HOLY ISLAND: *Major automatic (1977) lit 1905*
Position: *55°31.2′N 5°03.8′W*
Character: *Flashing 2 white every 20 seconds*
Nominal range: *25 miles*
Structure: *White square tower 23 metres high*
Foghorn: *2 4-second blasts every 90 seconds*

PLADDA: *Manned, lit 1790*
Position: *55°25.5′N 5°07.3′W*
Character: *Flashing 3 white every 30 seconds*
Nominal range: *23 miles*
Structure: *White tower 29 metres high*
Fog siren: *2 blasts every 20 seconds*

TURNBERRY: *Major automatic (1986) lit 1873*
Position: *55°19′N 4°50′W*
Character: *Flashing white every 15 seconds*
Nominal range: *22 miles*
Structure: *White tower 24 metres high, of scientific interest*

AILSA CRAIG: *See page 96*

CORSEWALL: *Manned, lit 1817*
Position: *55°00.5′N 5°09.5′W*
Character: *Alternate long flashing white and red every
74 seconds*
Nominal range: *18 miles*
Structure: *White tower 34 metres high*
Fog siren: *4 blasts every 90 seconds*

LOCH RYAN: *Major automatic (1964) lit 1847*
Position: *54°58.5′N 5°01.8′W*
Character: *Flashing 2 red every 10 seconds*
Nominal range: *12 miles*
Structure: *White tower 15 metres high*

KILLANTRINGAN: *See page 98*

CRAMMAG HEAD: *Major automatic*
Position: *54°39.9′N 4°57.8′W*
Character: *Flashing white every 10 seconds*
Nominal range: *18 miles*
Structure: *White tower 6 metres high*

MULL OF GALLOWAY: *See page 100*

ISLE OF MAN

POINT OF AYRE: *See page 102*

MAUGHOLD HEAD: *Manned, lit 1914*
Position: *54°18′N 4°19′W*
Character: *Flashing 3 white every 30 seconds*
Nominal range: *22 miles*
Structure: *White tower 23 metres high*
Fog siren: *Every 90 seconds*

DOUGLAS HEAD: *Manned, lit 1859 replacing tower
of 1832*
Position: *54°08.6′N 4°27.9′W*
Character: *Flashing white every 10 seconds*
Nominal range: *25 miles*
Structure: *White tower 20 metres high*

LANGNESS: *See page 104*

CHICKEN ROCK: *See page 106*

CALF OF MAN: *Manned, lit 1968. Original tower built
1818, discontinued 1875*
Position: *54°03.2′N 4°49.6′W*
Character: *Flashing white every 15 seconds*
Nominal range: *28 miles*
Structure: *White 8-sided tower on granite building,
11 metres high*
Foghorn: *1 blast of 2.5 seconds every 45 seconds*

EAST

ST ABB'S HEAD: *See page 108*

BASS ROCK: *See page 110*

INCHKEITH: *See page 112*

FIDRA: *Major automatic (1970) lit 1885*
Position: *56°04.4′N 2°47′W*
Character: *Flashing 4 white every 30 seconds*
Nominal range: *24 miles*
Structure: *White brick tower 17 metres high*

ISLE OF MAY: *See page 114*

ELIE NESS: *Major automatic*
Position: *56°11′N 2°48.6′W*
Character: *Flashing white every 6 seconds*
Nominal range: *18 miles*
Structure: *White tower 11 metres high*

FIFE NESS: *Built as a major automatic 1975*
Position: *56°16.7′N 2°35.1′W*
Character: *Iso white/red every 10 seconds*
Nominal range: *White 21 miles, red 20 miles*
Structure: *White building 5 metres high*

BELL ROCK: *See page 118*

SCURDIE NESS: *Manned, lit 1870*
Position: *56°42.1′N 2°26.1′W*
Character: *Flashing 3 white every 30 seconds*
Nominal range: *21 miles*
Structure: *White tower 39 metres high, of
architectural and historic interest*

TOD HEAD: *Manned, lit 1897*
Position: *56°53′N 2°12.8′W*
Character: *Flashing 4 white every 30 seconds*
Nominal range: *29 miles*
Structure: *White tower of architectural and historic interest*
Foghorn: *4 blasts every 60 seconds*

GIRDLE NESS: *See page 120*

BUCHAN NESS: *Manned, lit 1827*
Position: *57°28.2′N 1°46.4′W*
Character: *Flashing white every 5 seconds*
Nominal range: *28 miles*
Structure: *White tower 35 metres high with red bands; of
architectural and historic interest*
Fog siren: *3 blasts of 3 seconds every 90 seconds*

RATTRAY HEAD: *Major automatic (1982) lit 1895*
Position: *57°36.6′N 1°48.9′W*
Character: *Flashing 3 white every 30 seconds*
Nominal range: *24 miles*
Structure: *White tower of granite and brick 34 metres high,
of architectural and historic interest*
Foghorn: *2 blasts every 45 seconds*

KINNAIRD HEAD: *See page 122*

COVESEA SKERRIES: *See page 124*

CHANONRY: *Major automatic (1984) lit 1846*
Position: *57°34.5'N 4°05.4'W*
Character: *Occulting white every 6 seconds*
Nominal range: *15 miles*
Structure: *White tower 13 metres high, of architectural and historic interest*

CROMARTY: *Major automatic (1985) lit 1846*
Position: *54°41'N 4°02.1'W*
Character: *Occulting white/red every 10 seconds*
Nominal range: *White 14 miles, red 11 miles*
Structure: *White tower 13 metres high*

TARBAT NESS: *See page 125*

CLYTHNESS: *Major automatic (1964) lit 1916*
Position: *58°19'N 3°13'N*
Character: *Flashing 2 white every 30 seconds*
Structure: *White tower with red band, 13 metres high*

NOSS HEAD: *Manned, lit 1849*
Position: *58°28.8'N 3°03'W*
Character: *Flashing white/red every 20 seconds*
Nominal range: *White 25 miles, red 21 miles*
Structure: *White stone tower 18 metres high*

NORTH

CAPE WRATH: *See page 126*

STRATHY POINT: *Manned, lit 1958*
Position: *58°36'N 4°01'W*
Character: *Flashing white every 20 seconds*
Nominal range: *27 miles*
Structure: *Low white tower 14 metres high on white house*
Fog signal: *4 diaphone blasts every 90 seconds*

HOLBURN HEAD: *Manned, lit 1862*
Position: *58°36.9'N 3°32.4'W*
Character: *Flashing white/red every 10 seconds*
Nominal range: *White 15 miles, red 11 miles*
Structure: *White tower 17 metres high*
Fog siren: *Every 20 seconds*

DUNNET HEAD: *See page 128*

DUNCANSBY HEAD: *Manned, lit 1924*
Position: *58°38.6'N 3°01.4'W*
Character: *Flashing white every 12 seconds*
Nominal range: *24 miles*
Structure: *White tower 11 metres high*

STROMA: *See page 130*

ORKNEY

PENTLAND SKERRIES: *See page 132*

CANTICK HEAD: *Manned, lit 1858*
Position: *58°47.2'N 3°07.8'W*
Character: *Flashing white every 20 seconds*
Nominal range: *22 miles*
Structure: *White tower 22 metres high, of architectural and historic interest*
Foghorn: *2 blasts every 30 seconds*

HOY HIGH AND HOY LOW: *See page 138*

COPINSAY: *See page 136*

AUSKERRY: *Major automatic (1961) lit 1867*
Position: *59°01.6'N 2°34.2'W*
Character: *Flashing white every 20 seconds*
Nominal range: *18 miles*
Structure: *White tower 34 metres high*

HELLIAR HOLM: *Major automatic (1967) lit 1893*
Position: *59°01.2'N 2°54'W*
Character: *Flashing white/red/green every 10 seconds*
Nominal range: *White 14 miles, red 10 miles, green 10 miles*
Structure: *White tower 13 metres high*

BROUGH OF BIRSAY: *See page 144*

NOUP HEAD: *Major automatic (1964) lit 1898*
Position: *59°19.9'N 3°04'W*
Character: *Flashing white every 30 seconds*
Structure: *White tower 24 metres high*

SULE SKERRY: *See page 140*

START POINT: *See page 146*

NORTH RONALDSAY: *Manned, lit 1854, replacing previous tower 1789-1809*
Position: *59°23.4'N 2°22.8'W*
Character: *Flashing white every 10 seconds*
Nominal range: *19 miles*
Structure: *Redbrick tower 42 metres high, with 2 white bands*
Foghorn: *5 blasts every 60 seconds*

SHETLAND

FAIR ISLE SOUTH AND NORTH: *See page 148*

SUMBURGH HEAD: *See page 150*

BRESSAY: *Manned, lit 1858*
Position: *60°07.2'N 1°07.2'W*
Character: *Flashing 2 white every 30 seconds*
Nominal range: *21 miles*
Structure: *White tower 16 metres high*
Fog siren: *2 blasts every 90 seconds*

OUT SKERRIES: *See page 151*

FIRTH'S VOE: *Major automatic*
Position: *60°27.2'N 1°10.6'W*
Character: *Occulting white/red/green every 8 seconds*
Nominal range: *White 15 miles, red 10 miles, green 10 miles*
Structure: *White tower 8 metres high*

ESHA NESS: *Major automatic (1974) lit 1929*
Position: *60°29.3'N 1°37.6'W*
Character: *Flashing white every 12 seconds*
Nominal range: *25 miles*
Structure: *White square tower 12 metres high*

POINT OF FETHALAND: *Built as a major automatic 1977*
Position: *60°38.1°N 1°18.6'W*
Character: *Flashing 3 white/red every 15 seconds*
Nominal range: *White 24 miles, red 20 miles*
Structure: *White tower 7 metres high*

MUCKLE FLUGGA: *See page 152*

MINOR LIGHTHOUSES AND BEACONS

WEST	*Position*
Sula Sgeir	*59°05.6′N 6°09.5′W*
Carloway	*58°17′N 6°50′W*
Greinam	*58°13.3′N 6°46.2′W*
Milaid Point	*58°01′N 6°21.8′W*
Rubh Uisenis	*57°56.2′N 6°28.2′W*
Weaver Point	*57°36.6′N 7°05.8′W*
Calvay	*57°08.5′N 7°15.3′W*
Rubha Glas	*56°56.8′N 7°30.6′W*
Sgeir Leadh	*56°56.7′N 7°30.7′W*
Dubh Sgeir	*56°56.4′N 7°28.9′W*
Calleach Head	*57°55.8′N 5°24.1′W*
Rubha Cadail	*57°55.5′N 5°13.2′W*
Eilean Troddaý	*57°43.6′N 6°17.8′W*
Vaternish	*57°36.5′N 6°38′W*
Dunvegan	*57°26.8′N 6°36.5′W*
Ardtreck	*57°20.4′N 6°25.8′W*
Eyre Point	*57°20′N 6°01.3′W*
Crowlin	*57°21.3′N 5°51.3′W*
Kyleakin	*57°16.7′N 5°44.5′W*
Sgeir-na-Cailleach	*57°15.6′N 5°38.8′W*
Kylerhea	*57°14.2′N 5°39.9′W*
Ornsay Beacon	*57°08.6′N 5°46.4′W*
Sandaig: *See page 84*	
Sleat Point	*57°1′N 6°1′W*
Canna	*57°02.8′N 6°27.9′W*
Eigg	*56°32′N 6°7′W*
Corran	*56°43.3′N 5°14.5′W*
Corran Narrows	*56°43.6′N 5°13.8′W*
Cairns of Coll	*56°42.2′N 6°26.8′W*
Bunessan	*56°20.5′N 6°16.2′W*
Ardmore	*56°39.4′ 6°07.6′W*
Rubha nan Gall	*56°38.3′N 6°03.9′W*
Green Island	*56°32.3′N 5°54.7′W*
Ardtornish	*56°31.1′N 5°45.1′W*
Grey Rocks	*56°29.8′N 5°42.7′W*
Duart Point	*56°26.9′N 5°38.7′W*
Lady Rock	*56°27′N 5°37′W*
Sgeir Bhuidhe	*56°33.6′N 5°24.6′W*
Dunollie	*56°25.4′N 5°29′W*
North Spit of Kerrera	*56°25′N 5°29.5′W*
Dubh Sgeir, Kerrera Sound	*56°22.8′N 5°32.2′W*
Fladda: *See page 92*	
Dubh Sgeir, Luing	*56°14.8′N 5°40.1′W*
The Garvellachs	*56°13.1′N 5°48.9′W*
Scalasaig, Colonsay	*56°4′N 6°10.8′W*
Reisa an t'Sruith, Jura	*56°07.8′N 5°38.8′W*
Ruadh Sgeir	*56°04.3′N 5°39.7′W*
Skervuile	*55°52.5′N 5°49.8′W*
Eilean nan Gabhar	*55°50′N 5°56.2′W*
Na Cultean	*55°48.7′N 5°54.8′W*
Carragh an t-Sruith	*55°52.3′N 6°05.7′W*
Carrach Mhor	*55°50.4′N 6°6′W*
Loch Indaal	*55°44.7′N 6°22.4′W*
Port Ellen	*55°37.2′N 6°12.7′W*
Eilean a Chuirn	*55°40.2′N 6°01.1′W*
Lady Isle	*55°31.6′N 4°44′W*
Holy Island	*55°30.7′N 5°04.1′W*
Little Ross	*54°45.9′N 4°5′W*
Hestan Island	*54°50′N 3°48.4′W*

ISLE OF MAN	
Thousla Rock	*54°03.7′N 4°48′W*

EAST	
Barns Ness	*55°59.2′N 2°26.6′W*
Oxcars	*56°01.4′N 3°16.7′W*
Inchcolm	*56°01.7′N 3°17.7′W*
Cairnbulg Briggs	*57°41.1′N 1°56.4′W*
Longman Point	*57°30′N 4°13.2′W*
Craigton Point	*57°30.1′N 4°14.0′W*

NORTH	
Loch Eriboll	*58°31.1′N 4°38.8′W*

ORKNEY	
Lother Rock	*58°43.8′N 2°58.5′W*
Swona: *See page 134*	
Tor Ness	*58°46.7′N 3°17.6′W*
Ruff Reef	*58°47.5′N 3°07.8′W*
Hoxa Head	*58°49.3′N 3°2′W*
Roseness	*58°52.4′N 2°49.9′W*
Barrel of Butter	*58°53.4′N 3°07.5′W*
Cava	*58°53.2′N 3°10.6′W*
Skerry of Ness	*58°57′N 3°17.7′W*
Papa Stronsay	*59°09.3′N 2°34.8′W*
Calf Sound	*59°14.2′N 2°45.7′W*

SHETLAND	
Mousa	*59°59.8′N 1°09.4′W*
Fugla Ness	*60°06.4′N 1°20.7′W*
Rova Head	*60°11.5′N 1°08.5′W*
Vaila Sound	*60°12′N 1°33.4′W*
Mull of Eswick	*60°15.8′N 1°05.8′W*
Ve Skerries	*60°22.4′N 1°48.7′W*
Gruna Island	*60°39.2′N 1°18′W*
Muckle Roe	*60°21′N 1°26.9′W*
Symbister Ness	*60°20.5′N 1°02.1′W*
Skate of Marrister	*60°21.4′N 1°01.3′W*
Suther Ness	*60°22.2′N 1°0′W*
Muckle Skerry	*60°26.4′N 0°51.7′W*
Hillswick	*60°27.2′N 1°29.7′W*
Lunna Holm	*60°27.4′N 1°02.4′W*
Lamba South	*60°30.8′N 1°17.8′W*
Muckle Holm	*60°34.9′N 1°15.8′W*
Brother Isle	*60°30′N 1°13.9′W*
Ness of Sound	*60°31.4′N 1°11.1′W*
Quey Firth	*60°31.5′N 1°19.5′W*
Outer Skerry	*60°33.1′N 1°18.2′W*
Little Holm	*60°33.5′N 1°15.8′W*
Whitehill	*60°34.9′N 1°0.1′W*
Bagi Stack	*60°43.5′N 1°07.4′W*
Uyeasound	*60°41.2′N 0°55.3′W*
Balta Sound	*60°44.5′N 0°47.6′W*

BIBLIOGRAPHY

Headrick, Reverend James *General View of the Agriculture of the County of Angus or Forfarshire* Edinburgh 1813
Elliot, Major George H. *Report of a Tour of Inspection of European Lighthouse Systems made in 1873* Washington 1874
Tait, Thomas T. *Early History of Lighthouses* Glasgow 1902
Stevenson, D.A. *Report on Safety of Navigation, Lighted Buoys, 12th International Congress of Navigation, Philadelphia* Brussels 1912
Northern Lighthouse Journals 1967-86
Smout, T.C. *A History of the Scottish People 1560-1830* London 1969
Lillie, John Adam, QC *Tradition and Environment* Aberdeen 1970
Tennant, Charles *The Radical Laird: A Biography of George Kinloch 1775-1833* Kineton 1970
Chitnis, Annan C. *The Scottish Enlightenment* London 1976
Mair, Craig *A Star for Seamen: The Stevenson Family of Engineers* London 1978
Munro, R.W. *Scottish Lighthouses* Stornoway 1979
Scott, Sir Walter *Northern Lights: Or A Voyage in the Lighthouse Yacht to Nova Zembla and the Lord Knows Where in the Summer of 1814* (extract from Lockhart's *Life*) Hawick 1982
Whatley, C.A. *The Salt Industry and its Trade in Fife and Tayside c.1570-1850* Dundee 1984
University of Wales Maritime Ergonomics Research Unit *Ergonomic and Psychological Aspects of Lightkeeping* 1984 (unpublished)

INDEX OF NAMES